FAITH, FRIENDS, AND FESTIVAL QUEENS

CONFESSIONS of a
Not-So- SUPERMODEL

BROOKLYN LINDSEY

 ZONDERVAN®

ZONDERVAN.com/
AUTHORTRACKER
follow your favorite authors

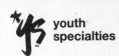 youth
specialties

youth specialties

Confessions of a Not-So-Supermodel
Copyright 2008 by Brooklyn Lindsey

Youth Specialties products, 300 S. Pierce St., El Cajon, CA 92020 are published by Zondervan, 5300 Patterson Ave. SE, Grand Rapids, MI 49530.

Library of Congress Cataloging-in-Publication Data

Lindsey, Brooklyn.
  Confessions of a not-so-supermodel : faith, friends, and festival queens / Brooklyn Lindsey.
      p. cm.
ISBN-10: 0-310-27753-1 (pbk.)
ISBN-13: 978-0-310-27753-8 (pbk.)
  1. Teenage girls—Religious life—Juvenile literature. 2. Self-perception in adolescence—Religious aspects—Christianity—Juvenile literature. I. Title.
  BV4551.3.L56 2008
  248.8'33—dc22

                                                                2007041816

Cover and Interior design by SharpSeven Design

Printed in the United States of America

08 09 10 11 12 13 • 18 17 16 15 14 13 12 11 10 9 8 7 6 5 4 3 2 1

To our daughter, Kirra,

who was with me every moment of this journey.

You are a dream I never could have imagined.

ACKNOWLEDGMENTS

I raise my glass (of hot pink fruit punch)...

To the girls of Central Florida and DFW Texas. You've made me a "supermodel."

To my love, Coy, who suffered valiantly through my writing, working, and being pregnant at the same time. Your sharp mind, compassionate heart, and quick humor give me energy and strength.

To Jen, who planned my future with Coy during a youth workers' convention. Your friendship and motivation led me here.

To Jay and David, two who believed in this Appalachian heiress.

To Doug, Becca, Karen, and Holly, my invaluable editors.

To Dave and Kelly, for making great lives for us kids. Thanks for encouraging me to participate in The Parade of the Hills.

To Delbert and Natalie, for loving me like one of their own.

To Grandma. Your dreams encouraged mine.

To my siblings. You are amazing. Thanks for loving me.

To the O'Connors, for getting me through the rough patches and for making homemade guacamole. "Y'all" are fabulous.

To Christy. I can never repay you for believing in me.

To the WC girls. Your spiritual beauty has left an awesome tattoo on my life.

To Terrell Sanders at MVNU. Your encouragement led me to believe I could write someday.

To our real-life baby doll, Kirra. I finished the first draft of this book three days before you were born, and made revisions while holding you in my arms. You've helped me understand what it really means to have a dream come true. I hope you'll grow to understand and embrace your own royal lineage.

And, finally, to the tiny town of Nelsonville, Ohio, to the organizers of The Parade of the Hills, and to all the queens who travel the OFEA circuit. You are beautiful. May God bless each of you with dreams that lead to true fulfillment.

TABLE OF CONTENTS

A Dream, a Crown, and a Twisted Ankle 11

Festival Queens 31

Parades 42

Platform...49

People 56

Presents 67

A Wandering Queen 75

Faith and Fruit...81

Rumors 89

Replacement 100

Risk..108

Royalty 115

Friends...123

Add Me 132

Love Me..142

Love You 154

That's What Dreams Are Made of...................163

A DREAM, A CROWN, AND A TWISTED ANKLE

CONFESSION: WHEN I WAS LITTLE, I THOUGHT THAT IF I SWALLOWED A WATERMELON SEED, IT WOULD TURN INTO A BABY IN MY BELLY AND MAKE ME PREGNANT. I ALSO THOUGHT I MIGHT GROW UP TO BE A SUPERMODEL SOMEDAY. LATER I LEARNED THAT SWALLOWING A WATERMELON SEED IS HARMLESS AND WILL LEAD TO NOTHING MORE THAN SOME MILD INDIGESTION. I ALSO LEARNED THAT A TATTERED AND FRAYED GIRL LIKE ME IS BETTER SUITED FOR RUNWAYS THAT ARE NOT SO GLAMOROUS.

Perhaps you're wondering who the enchanting beauty queen on the previous page is. You know—the one with the stylish pink dress and the not-so-stylish bandage on her twisted ankle.

CONFESSIONS OF A Not-So- SUPERMODEL

Well, that's me.

The photo was taken in the fall of 1996. I was sitting on top of a luxury car as I rode through a small-town festival parade. It was my senior year in high school, and I was a festival queen—a far cry from the supermodel lifestyle I'd once dreamt about. The stylish supermodels of the 90s—Nikki Taylor, Cindy Crawford, Tyra Banks—were people whose lifestyles I sought after. But somehow, through a weird chain of events, I ended up sitting atop a car as a festival queen.

It's obvious I'm no supermodel. Unless you count my dog, no one thinks I'm famous. No one has ever followed me around desperately trying to snap a picture of me as I dine at

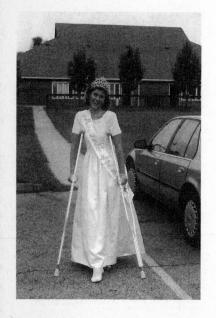

a ritzy restaurant or carry my grocery bags into my house. In fact, when compared side by side, the dreams of my youth and the realities of my life seem as different as Sanjaya Malakar and Carrie Underwood. But I'm guessing that if these two *American Idol* stars wanted to, they could pull off a pretty decent duet, in spite of their obvious differences in style and musical genre.

It's the same for me as I look at the differences between the life I'd imagined as a supermodel and the indisputable gift that is my own "super-model" life. When I became a festival queen and, later on, a youth pastor, one might think I didn't make it, that I wasn't any kind of supermodel at all. But I have become one—in a wonderful, different, unexpected Sanjaya-and-Carrie type of way.

I write to you, beautiful young friend, because not so long ago I was a teenager like you, searching for something to give my life meaning and purpose, and wishing for someone to love me. In my journey I found something I think will be worth your time, something that could change the way you look at yourself and the direction of your own dreams.

TRIPPED UP

A few years ago I was on my way home from a National Youth Worker's Convention and had some time before my flight. I was wandering around an airport bookstore when I stumbled onto something that would eventually lead me here, writing to you. Now when I say "stumbled," I mean it literally—I tripped over my little travel suitcase and went hurtling into a display at the Hudson News Bookstore in the airport in Columbus, Ohio. Not only did I scatter the display and send about ten books to new homes on the floor, but I also ended up on the ground myself, scrambling after the books I'd just knocked over. There probably weren't many people watching, but I was embarrassed—so I picked up one of the books I'd landed on and pretended to studiously read the back cover.

That book had a profound impact on me. It was called *Ophelia Speaks: Adolescent Girls Write about Their Search for Self*

(Harper, 1999). It was written by a college student named Sara Shandler who'd begun working on it when she was just 16. Shandler's book was a response to another book written five years earlier, Mary Pipher's *Reviving Ophelia: Saving the Selves of Adolescent Girls* (Riverhead, 1994). Both books were about girls and the challenges they face, but Sara Shandler got the stories straight from other young women like her who were in the midst of the struggle. The idea intrigued me. The young women in Shandler's book shared about the difficult issues shaping their lives—ranging from family dysfunction to drug abuse, friendship to eating disorders. I read each chapter with tears in my eyes, marveling at the harsh realities girls face each day and wondering where they find hope. I was saddened and frustrated that there were very few glimmers of healing to be found in the book, very little evidence of wholeness.

The hope I did see sprang from the honesty of the girls willing to share their stories. Sharing a story can be healing in itself, a freedom someone experiences when something pent-up gets set free. But something major was still missing. As the author wrote of the thousands of stories that had poured in for this book, I thought of all the young women who had written, desperately desiring to be heard. Although it wasn't the purpose of her book, I wished Shandler had included the stories of the girls who had found wholeness and strength through the struggle, the ones who had found redemption and forgiveness. As I thought about how I'd wandered through the murkiness of adolescence, I realized the girls in the book—and the girls I minister to back home—were all wandering, too. They hadn't yet found that they could emerge from the wilderness into a land of purpose and plenty.

I shared this observation with the girls at the camp I attended every summer. I read a few of the stories from the book with them, and told them how I wished it had included stories of hope and inspiration in the midst of those same struggles. I longed to read of the girl who—through the struggle, after the tragedy, in the midst of darkness—found a new reason to live. I longed to read of the girl who suffered pain or obsession but found that light and transformation were available to her. I wasn't looking for every story to turn out perfectly in the end. I was looking for the stories of girls who didn't have a perfect life but were willing to live by faith and to chase after their God-given dreams anyway.

I guess I was looking for a story more like mine. I once lived in darkness. I once lived with fears and dysfunctions—in fact, I still do. But God brought me into a place of light, a place where I could deal with these struggles in a way that reveals the person God desires me to be.

I grew up in a state of semi-confusion and youthful hope about my dreams. I would stare into my bedroom mirror, envisioning myself as a runway model—believing that if I worked hard enough, I could become the next great supermodel. But this dream also scared me. I would have died if I ever found someone spying on me as I posed in the mirror. I held these dreams of my heart tight inside, fearing that if I revealed them to anyone, then I might be held accountable to them or be seen as a failure if things didn't work out. In my mind it was better to be safe and keep my hopes and dreams to myself than to share my dreams and be let down in front of everyone.

It's not easy to be a teenage girl. I'm sure you have your own struggles. Struggles (plural) camped out in my teenage mind and body for a long time, and I didn't even realize how some of these struggles were damaging my understanding of myself and even my relationships. So, after reading a book about girls I didn't know and considering my own story, I had to ask...

...Is there anyone else? Is there anyone else who has been able to find her way through the struggles that keep her from seeing who they are in Christ and the dreams God has given her? I had to believe there were others who had seen the truths beyond all of the lies. There have to be others who, in the midst of struggle, have found a new reason to be alive.

I brought all these thoughts to the girls at camp that summer. I told them I wanted to find the girls who recognized God in the midst of their circumstances (even during the most painful and unjust ones), to share the stories of girls who were in the heat of life but were holding on to something far more stable than their temporary and sometimes false selves. I wanted to offer a sequel of sorts—one that showed resilience and strength gained from having a relationship with Christ through even the hardest times.

After my talk that day, I hung out at the front of the room among metal folding chairs while sounds of lunch being prepared rang in the nearby kitchen. I expected all the girls to exit the room where we met, but instead a line of girls formed in front of me. Each one of them had something unique to share with me, her own story of hope. One girl, Natasha, urged me with fiery determination to never stop believing in this dream to help girls find their voices for God. I will never forget what she said to me, "Pastor Brook, I'm going to write that book for you someday." She was talking about a book in which she would share her struggle and how God gave her strength to get though it. She was determined to find a way to share her story of hope and redemption with others.

Who knows what Natasha is up to today? Maybe she's working on writing that book. Or maybe she doesn't even remember that little talk we had that afternoon in the heat of summer. But I know I felt deeply her strong desire to be heard, and it reinvigorated my belief that God is at work in all of us. And it made me want to tell my own story.

So here I am, writing a book I dreamed about years ago, and telling you I wasn't always so sure of myself. I sit here a few months away from giving birth to a daughter of my own, and I wonder, "How on earth am I going to say anything that makes a difference to you?" But it's the same feeling I had that day at camp when sharing my heart with young girls yielded great fruit. So I'm trusting that something good will happen again. I'm hoping you will read something here that will speak to your heart and help you realize how awesome you are in God's sight.

I dreamt about being a supermodel my entire life. Now I know what that dream was for. It led me here, to this place of sharing with you.

SUPERMODEL BABY

We don't usually categorize babies as supermodels. So to say that I was born with a supermodel birthmark, or something that set me apart to become a model, really wouldn't be fair. But as far back as I can remember, I daydreamed about becoming a supermodel.

Brooke Shields was perhaps the most famous model of my childhood days, and I knew she'd been modeling since she was a very young girl. I believed there was a supermodel living in me, too. I even had a book about Brooke, filled with pictures of her when she was young. The pages were worn, and I'd read the beauty tips over and over again. I still remember most of them: "Always throw away mascara after six weeks." "Wash your face each night." "Don't pick!" The similarities in our names (Brooke/

Brooklyn) just added to my hopes of being like her someday. I even had bushy eyebrows like hers (which were totally in style in the early 1990s).

I landed my first "gig" in front of the camera when I was just a month old. Of course, it wasn't really modeling—it was just a formal photo shoot for a baby portrait like so many

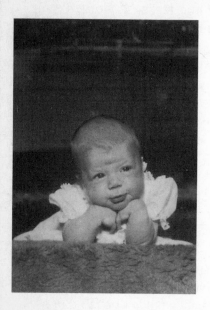

parents are more than happy to pay for. But that picture generated a story that would help me believe modeling was in my future. My loving parents took me to a photographer who discovered I was very flexible, like Gumby from the Claymation show I used to watch on TV. So the photographer positioned my hands under my chin, ran over to the camera, and snapped the picture before I completely lost circulation in my tiny wrists and toppled over onto the velvet-rug-mountain thing I was propped up on. The moment was perfect, producing a picture where I looked stable and in control. It was clear that I was a prodigy, a natural in front of the camera!

This early display of flexibility and camera-friendliness on the rug mountain was the beginning of my modeling dream. Growing up, people told me I was photogenic and that I should consider a career in modeling. I loved it when folks would compliment my height or my green eyes. My grandma was especially supportive of my hopes to become a model. She affirmed my intelligence, my personality, and my appearance, helping me believe I could be a big-time model someday.

I started modeling for an agency at the age of 10. Grandma would drive me 45 minutes into the city for short photo shoots, and I would stare out the window wondering how I became so lucky.

As I look back at the pictures, it's clear that some of the advertisements I did back then weren't the coolest. I remember one photo shoot where I wore an orange-and-navy-blue striped jumpsuit and pretended to talk on a telephone. Most of the ads were cheesy—far from the more professional shots you might see in *Vanity Fair*. In fact, I always thought my best shoot was the one at the very beginning when I was a baby propped up on a rug. I like to think it reflects the real me, the one who hadn't been shaped by the world's expectations yet. It's a little embarrassing to admit, but I still like getting this old baby picture out and admiring it. I wasn't worried then about what I was wearing or what was holding me up. The picture was a true reflection of the person I was becoming—the person I was proud to be.

Babies and little kids are comfortable with who they are. They don't worry about what other people are thinking. I wish things could stay that way. I wish we could continue living in a state of contentment, unmarked by the critique of others. I wish our dreams and confidence in who we are could stay intact. But normally that doesn't happen. Instead, as we grow up, we begin seeing ourselves in comparison to those around us.

THE SUPERMODEL DREAM

The images I saw on TV as a kid encouraged girls to be beauties and princesses. I wanted to be those things; but I wanted to be other things too. I secretly liked "boy shows" like *Transformers* and *Thundercats*. But I knew that if I didn't submit to girl callings, I might miss out on the dream.

CONFESSIONS OF A Not-So-SUPERMODEL

As a teenager, media outlets like MTV and teen magazines reinforced this desire to fit into the girl world, which always reassured my ambitions to become a supermodel. The world loves this type of girl: Why would I want to be anything else?

Here's the message I was hearing and believing: "If you are young, beautiful, and in front of the camera, your life will be filled with happiness, love, and money! Could anything be better?" At the time the world's sales pitch had me convinced there was nothing better than "having it all" (good looks, a successful modeling career, acceptance from the world, and a nice paycheck to buy more stuff). What I didn't know was that my ambition to become a supermodel would fuel an unhealthy image of myself and create an emptiness I didn't really know how to fill.

People have to make sacrifices to attain their dreams. Living out a dream requires faithfulness and an unwavering persistence that keeps you from giving up. The really great athletes in my high school class didn't divide their time up among an assortment of different sports and clubs. They focused on the one thing that gave them the most joy. They were passionate about training and didn't quit when they got discouraged. My friends who have become doctors and lawyers gave up lots of time and money (and sleep) to live their dreams. Aspiring writers may dream of winning a Pulitzer Prize—but before the awards start pouring in, they've usually had to hold on when the pay was small and the accolades nonexistent. So I shouldn't have been surprised that becoming a supermodel would take every ounce of courage and faith I could find.

Courage isn't really a problem when you are a month old and you don't know any better than to just be who you are. But what happens when we become aware that we live in a world marked by social status, cliques, and popularity? What happens when we become aware that other people are watching us and perhaps even judging us? For me, this realization happened right before middle school, and it made me reevaluate my abilities as a future model.

MIDDLE SCHOOL TATTOOS: AWKWARDNESS THAT LEFT A MARK

I wish someone could have warned me about the fifth and sixth grades. Like many other people, I experienced these years as a frightening and awkward period when nothing looked proportional, pretty, or put together. During this time, I took to heart every comment about my looks, my personality, and my qualifications for popularity.

Even in the midst of this time of great physical and social awkwardness, I was doing print-ad modeling. I continued to get phone calls from the modeling agency. It was steady work for a time. My parents were very proud of me. My grandma was very dedicated and would pick me up and drive me to the photo shoots. During our rides to the city, she taught me many wonderful things. But there was one thing I had to learn on my own: that my longing for happiness, security, and self-worth would never be satisfied by modeling alone.

Each modeling success brought me a time of happiness, but these moments never delivered lasting fulfillment. Nonetheless, I held on to the hope that modeling might provide all I needed. Gracing the cover of *Vogue* was still a dream in my heart. But slowly things began to change.

Over the course of my middle school years, feelings of awkwardness and uncertainty began taking over my life. It was like someone turned on one of those giant fog machines you see at concerts—the ones that fill the stage with smoke until it surrounds everyone on the floor. There were moments as a young teenager when I couldn't see a thing, and I had no choice but to stand frozen in the middle of it. Sometimes the fog would clear for a little while, but just as I'd start to make sense of my surroundings, another blast of fog would cloud everything again.

The fog came in all kinds of shapes and sizes. There was the boy fog, the hair fog, the make-up fog, the parent fog, the grade fog, the teacher fog, the friend fog, the friend-turned-boyfriend fog, the "who will I room with during the winter retreat?" fog, the clothing fog, and many others. You've probably experienced this yourself. We all go through times when it's hard to see who we are and the dreams God has for us. Sometimes the fog will lift for a while and you can get a glimpse of the real you, but then it settles in again, and all is unclear.

Somewhere in the middle of the fog, my modeling dream was still there. I could still catch a glimpse of it from time to time, but my self-consciousness and feelings of inadequacy wouldn't let me see the full picture anymore. I had the support of my family, but they needed my enthusiasm to continue—they couldn't make me continue modeling or make me want to go further. After a few brief years of modeling, I didn't feel very comfortable with it anymore. I felt uneasy in front of the camera and shy about being photographed. It didn't help that I was getting taller and clumsier. With the sixth grade came braces and some really freaky side bangs (which didn't help my self-confidence or my belief that I was getting closer to a Brooke Shields existence). I could barely see the dream through the fog, and it was discouraging. On days when I had a shoot, I'd be filled with this contradictory mixture of excitement and dread—though

I could never really say what I was dreading. So my modeling work tapered off, as did my interest in continuing.

Eventually, I stopped accepting calls from my agency and didn't do any modeling work for quite a while. I was okay with this. I didn't have to worry about the anxiety of performing anymore. I spent my time doing other things. I practiced volleyball, spent time with friends, listened to music, and talked on the phone. Modeling—and the dream that went with it—faded into the background.

It wasn't until my senior year in high school that the dream popped up again in the form of another modeling opportunity. My mom took me into Columbus, Ohio, to be seen by a modeling agency. I walked down a short runway as experts critiqued everything from my look (hair, face, body, height, weight—you name it!) to my confidence level. Then, the coolest thing happened. I was offered a chance to go to New York City to establish myself as a model!

But something inside me said "no." It was that same fear, something I couldn't explain, that surfaced again and made me shrink back. My mom was willing to help me do whatever it took. But there was something missing, and I just couldn't follow through. I felt unsure about the whole thing, so I allowed another opportunity to fade.

Late in high school I discovered a relationship with Jesus Christ, and this relationship began to inform my understanding of life and its purpose. By the time I headed off to college, I knew I wanted to help people. I knew God had a special calling just for me. But how did my dream of becoming a model fit into that calling? I didn't know, so I buried the dream under a busy school schedule, volunteerism, and athleticism—knowing all along that a modeling career was something I still wished could happen.

Burying something doesn't necessarily mean that it goes away in a person's mind and heart. Today, I look back on those days and I can see what my problem was. I wasn't living. I was just surviving. I was empty inside, searching for something to fill the hole that the modeling dream had left in my life.

I think of those times when we are caught between believing in our dreams and being frustrated by them as times of wandering. We find ourselves journeying through a wilderness, uncertain of the path that leads to the clearing. We're searching for something that will fulfill and sustain us, but we aren't sure which berries along the path are poisonous and which are good. I was eager to find a way out of the wilderness I'd wandered into. I was looking for something that would give my life meaning—but that something I'd always thought would give me meaning (modeling) now scared the life out of me.

When we're lost in the brush of life, unsure about the direction we should head, sometimes we freeze—paralyzed by our fears. We give up pursuing our dreams and instead chase anything we think might give sustenance to our souls and direction to our hearts. I tried to fill up my soul with friends, with parties, with boys, and with honors. I never understood that I was getting nowhere, just wandering around in a big circle.

Have you ever felt this way? Have you ever felt like you had a dream that was impossible to achieve, and trying to chase it just frightened you? Some people are gifted with great confidence in their dreams. But most of us are not so sure of ourselves. And even the people who possess the most confidence still doubt sometimes. So what do we do? Where do we turn when we are directionally challenged? Where do we turn when we've met a dead end? Where do we turn when we are exhausted and not sure of the path to start down?

I suggest we need to start over. And I think the place to begin again is with our dreams.

We have to recognize the dreams God has planted within us. Those God-given dreams can be easily confused with other desires that might come to us from others or our own selfish ambitions. For example, there was a time in my childhood when I thought I wanted to become a dentist. I had a classmate whose dad was a dentist, and she always had really nice things. Now, to be honest, I hate the dentist. (Well, not *my* dentist, he's actually really nice.) But the thought of someone drilling into my teeth or scraping at them with a metal hook that looks like it can pierce my cheek freaks me out. Becoming a dentist was never God's dream for me; it was something I thought I wanted because it might bring me a big house with a pool and a yard and maybe even a cool little fire pit to roast marshmallows.

The dreams God plants in our souls are closely related to the gifts we've been born with, the gifts we should develop and pay attention to. Often, it's these gifts and strengths that lead to our dreaming (especially when we are children and uninhibited by the world's understanding of success). Knowing God loves you and created you with dreams and gifts is a good start to finding your way out of the wilderness. Knowing God is working in and through you right now to bring to life something amazing for our world is even better. But getting to that point may require that we deconstruct the way we see ourselves.

It's kind of like looking at your life as a Lego creation. You can take it apart to see how it was all put together, and then put it back again with the new knowledge you have. In the end, all the same pieces are there. Most likely, though, your new creation will look different from when you started.

Some time around the fifth or sixth grade, I began basing my sense of self-worth and success more and more on what other people thought of me. Temporary and unstable peer-directed goals were slowly replacing the gifts, plans, and purposes God had given me. I was doing things to gain approval from others, and my "dream" was to be viewed as talented and successful. My life was a tall, unstable Lego tower reaching toward the sky. (Think Leaning Tower of Pisa here, except more likely to fall over.) The good in me was barely visible, because it was covered by a false self that wasn't me—it was a version of me defined by everyone else.

Deconstructing my Lego-tower life took a long time, because the building had settled and had been sitting the same way for quite some time. However, when I finally took the tower apart and saw all the good pieces I had to work with, I was able to build a new construction. Instead of an unstable tower easily toppled by any toddler or small puppy, I became an elegant one-story fine arts building full of all kinds of beautiful, wonderful, and different pieces. Instead of a tower—where my gifts and joys were piled atop each other so those on the bottom were buried so deeply I forgot they were even there—I became an open space where God could move things around and move in me freely.

As you go through this process of deconstruction and reconstruction, you'll begin to see yourself and your dreams in a different light, a light not so scary. And you may find that your dreams, seen in this new light, don't look exactly like you thought they would. My supermodel dream became very different once I fully embraced the knowledge that I was a beloved child of God created for a purpose. The dream, in essence, was the same.

It just came into the world in a different way. Instead of my dream coming into the world by way of the modeling runways of New York or Paris, it came into the world via ministry to girls (a ministry you are a part of as you read this book).

So that's why you haven't heard the name Brooklyn Lindsey. Most supermodels are seen in magazines, on television, in fashion shows, on the runway, or at least in the occasional Guess jeans ad. But you won't find me there. You're more likely to see me at the local pizza joint, at Starbucks typing on my computer, or sharing a Frappuccino with students. You may see me in Victoria's Secret—but only when I have a coupon for a free lip-gloss or something.

I've become a supermodel in a different world, a world governed by different rules. I'm still walking a modeling runway, but it's different from the one I dreamed of as a young girl. My runway is long, and I've tripped in my metaphorical stilettos more than once. Regardless, I'm still hiking it, one foot after the other, moving toward what I've always wanted to be—original. Life is my runway, and hopefully if I get the "walk" down, it will be an example for girls to see and learn from. Today, my understanding of what it means to be a supermodel is completely different from what I imagined back in sixth grade. Let's just say that I've become a more literal interpretation of the word. The traditional definition of *supermodel* is far from the realities we know. (For example, Gisele Bundchen is a supermodel, and many of us are like her...minus the perfect curves, face, clothes, and million-dollar bank accounts!) I am part of a new breed of supermodels—a group you can be a part of if you desire.

LIVING THE DREAM

There is something deep inside me that has always told me I am special, loved, and unique. That same something is in each of us, but often it tends to lie just below the surface, waiting for us to respond. It's the knowledge of God's love and work in our lives. But just because we know God loves us doesn't mean that we believe it or respond to it. It can be hard to really believe that you are loved when Abercrombie tells you you're really not that beautiful unless your perfectly sun-kissed hair is streaming across your face as your swimsuit-perfect body floats away in a boat with a beautiful guy. Trying to find such confidence when growing up can be like searching for your earring on the bathroom floor when you are late for school. We struggle to see what we're looking for because we're in such a rush, in such a race, it's hard to slow down and find what we really need. I didn't know many people growing up who were 100 percent sure of themselves every day. But there is something unique in each one of us—something special that should make us proud and even excited about our futures. But it often lies dormant because we are all trying to fix the outside and make ourselves into little clones of one another. Each commercial, each TV show, and each magazine fashion tip moves us further and further from the knowledge God has been whispering in our ears.

Maybe you've never heard these messages from God. I started listening, really listening, when I was about your age. I started paying attention to the little things that God had placed in my life as indications of who I really am and what direction I should go. Finally, I realized that the chewing gum of the world had lost its flavor, and I was ready for something more lasting.

This book is about finding what is lasting. It's about finding the real you, the person you are in Christ, who is right there with you on the journey. It's about the hope that comes in remembering that you are God's beloved child. It's about learning to recognize God in your everyday life—which is essential to understanding what living in freedom is all about. The Bible tells us, "It is for freedom that Christ has set us free. Stand firm, then, and do not let yourselves be burdened again by a yoke of slavery" (Galatians 5:1). As we explore what living a life of freedom means, we'll tackle some tough questions. And, hopefully, we'll begin to develop some answers.

As you read this book, I hope you will find yourself taking a good look at your life with Christ, the friends you surround yourself with, and the dreams God is forming in you right now. You can live those dreams.

I know, because I'm living mine.

YOUR CONFESSIONS

Use these questions for group discussion or personal reflection:

What was your childhood dream? Is it still a dream now?

What images do the words "wilderness" and "wandering" evoke for you? What wilderness times have you experienced in your life?

What kind of "fogs" and distractions most often cloud your world? What clouds your view of your dreams? How about your view of your relationship with God?

Describe your Lego life. What kind of building would it be? What do the rooms look like? Does your life need a major renovation?

The Bible says, "Trust in the Lord with all your heart and lean not on your own understanding" (Proverbs 3:5). Do you feel like you can trust God with your dreams? Why or why not?

FESTIVAL QUEENS

CONFESSION: SOME OF THE MOST MEMORABLE MOMENTS OF
MY HIGH SCHOOL YEARS—AND SOME OF THE MOST AWKWARD
ONES—WERE EXPERIENCED WHILE WEARING A LARGE TIARA.
(MINE WEIGHED ABOUT 10 POUNDS AND LEFT A NICE
INDENTATION IN MY FOREHEAD.)

When I was 17 years old, I signed up for a beauty pageant. It was actually a "festival queen" competition. There are many such competitions in the state of Ohio—more than you might imagine. These local festivals don't get much national attention. But to the towns that started them, they are a big deal—a sacred tradition that happens every year.

In case you've never seen a festival queen competition, take some time to picture in your mind the Miss USA or Miss America contest. Imagine the lights, the shiny floor, the glowing contestants, the thousands of viewers, maybe a famous band or singer, and some celebrity emcees. Got the picture?

Now forget everything you just imagined except for the contestants, and add some outdoor grass-like carpet, some metal stairs (appropriate for getting heels stuck in), a single microphone, and some wicker fan chairs. This is the setting of a hometown festival.

I guarantee that wherever you live, there is a festival of some sort, named and revered for its signature "thing," and there is a queen who represents you and your town or city every year. (If you don't believe me, look it up online. Go ahead, I'll wait for you to get back...)

The Parade of the Hills is an annual festival that takes place every August in Nelsonville, Ohio, near where I was raised. It's been going for more than 50 years; in fact, my mom participated in the festival queen competition back when she was in high school. (If you want to read more about this festival, check it out on the Web at www.paradeofthehills.org.)

Now I didn't really want to run for festival queen. I was an active volleyball player, a busy older sister (chauffeuring my siblings to various functions), and a college hopeful. I knew that there were festivals all over the state of Ohio and, if I were to be elected queen of my hometown festival, I'd be expected to attend as many other festivals as I could. The last thing I wanted to do was spend my senior year of high school traveling all over the state of Ohio.

Despite my concerns about the yearlong traveling commitment, I felt like I should give the festival competition a try, mostly to make my family proud. I was pretty sure I wouldn't win. I was kind of an oddball, and I lived about 30 miles outside Nelsonville. (Most other contestants were hometown girls.) So I decided to make the most of the competition week by having fun, being myself, getting to know the other girls. It wasn't about winning. It was about representing my family and having a good time.

Here's what my week of competition for Parade of the Hills festival queen looked like:

Monday: Contestant picnic, swim party, tour of Rocky Boots shoe factory, train ride

Tuesday: Interviews (live on local TV), formalwear competition

Friday: Finalists announced on stage

Saturday: Parade of finalists and coronation of new queen

To my surprise, it really was a fun week. The folks in Nelsonville were so sweet and I enjoyed getting to know new people. But I was pretty sure I'd blown any chance of winning the crown during my televised interview.

The interview started out okay. I was asked, "If you could go back in time and visit with any person, who would it be?"

My first thought was Dr. Martin Luther King, Jr. I honestly didn't know a whole lot about him—but I knew he'd stood up for his beliefs in a way I really respected. I said I would have asked him what fueled his passion. I would have wanted to know how his faith in Christ led to his being a civil rights activist. *So far so good,* I thought.

The interview continued to go well until something unexpected happened.

The judges asked me to do an impersonation.

Yes, an impersonation. And I went into "freak-out mode." If you've ever been called on in class to answer a question from a homework assignment you didn't do, then you know what freak-out mode is. Well, freak-out mode took over, and I lost my mind at that point.

I can't remember if they requested Donald Duck, or if it was just the first thing I thought of. But before I knew it I was performing a finger/mouth/spit combo reenactment of what I thought Donald Duck might sound like. We all were laughing, and I'm sure they humored me more than I deserved. But at that point, it was certain in my mind. I was completely insane—and surely unfit for any jeweled crown.

That evening we all had to vote for who should be named Miss Congeniality. (I voted for my friend Marcy.) And then I walked in an aquamarine-sequined mermaid-like dress for the formal competition.

On Saturday, about 30 queens from other Ohio festivals showed up and greeted us. I met some queens I'd never heard of before: The Gourd Queen, the Melon Queen, the Ice Cream Queen, the Turkey Queen, the Dam Days Queen, the First Town

Days Queen, the Pumpkin Queen, the Tomato Queen, the Bratwurst Queen, the Paul Bunyan Queen (who had to carry an ax everywhere she went!), and many others.

The final moments of the competition were spent sitting in a white convertible, as my dad proudly drove me down Washington Street to the stage where the week's events would culminate with the crowning of the new queen. Riding through the streets, I started to feel a bit apprehensive. It was sort of like having "butterflies" in your stomach—except not as sweet. Perhaps they were hungry butterflies with giant piranha teeth. Whatever it was, it wasn't a good feeling, and it made me sweat in my sparkly dress. The possibility that I might actually win something in the competition was starting to sink in.

I knew my senior year of high school was already going to be busy. If I won this contest, I'd have to travel (with chaperones) nearly every weekend to a different festival. There was a small scholarship provided to the winner, but that didn't keep me from thinking about the time commitment. I began really hoping I wouldn't win.

I stepped out of the convertible with help from escorts. Most of the other girls had arrived before me and were already seated in folding chairs on the stage waiting for the ceremony to get started. I was escorted up the narrow metal stairs to my row. I sat next to Marcy, and we smiled out over the crowd of more than 5,000 loving Nelsonville folk, as we patiently waved the summer humidity and mosquitoes away from our faces.

Through our smiles was a conversation that sounded something like this:

Me: "I hope you win."

Marcy: "I hope you win."

Me: "No, I *really* hope I don't win."

Marcy: "I know. I'm not sure about this anymore."

Me: "I'm freaking out."

Marcy: "What did we get ourselves into?"

Me: "If we win, we'll have to travel all year. I don't know any of the other queens."

Still smiling wildly, the two of us stared into space, wondering what was to come and whether the temperature could get any hotter. We watched the crowd thicken on the streets as the reigning queen and her court said their final goodbyes. Then the announcement of this year's winners began. The first announcement was Miss Congeniality. I held my breath as a name was announced:

"Brooklyn Alvis."

Gulp.

That would be me.

I stood and received a sash, a plaque, and some flowers, and had my picture taken. It was such an honor to be chosen by the other contestants. I was so happy—I couldn't believe the other girls had voted for me. I was relieved as I sat down, feeling loved and proud.

Then it was time to announce the winner of the formalwear competition. I was still thinking about how great it was to be selected as Miss Congeniality when my name was called again! Not only had I been named Miss Congeniality, but I'd also been honored with an award that represented elegance and poise. I was both thankful and shocked at having won these fine awards. I stood there stunned as I listened to the cheers from my family and friends roll down the streets. And I wanted to jump up and down with joy, because I *knew* that since I'd won both of these titles, there was *no way* I was going to be selected festival queen. With two plaques in hand, I sat down, overjoyed to have been part of the event, delighted with the honors I'd won, and relieved I wouldn't be required to make the yearlong commitment.

Then it was time to crown the festival queen. The second runner-up was announced: Tawny.

Then the first runner-up was announced, my friend Marcy.

And finally, the 1996-1997 Miss Parade of the Hills was called out...

Brooklyn Alvis.

Me again.

CONFESSIONS OF A Not-So-SUPERMODEL

First thought: *What the heck?* Second thought: *Oh, wow, did they really choose me?* Third thought: *Stand up and receive your crown! Everyone is cheering for you—you're frozen. Move it!*

I sat with my face in my hands. How on earth could this be possible? I'd practically spit all over the judges during my Donald Duck impersonation! I'd already won the other two titles!

But I stood up as the former queen placed that beautiful but heavy crown on my head...

The next year taught me a great deal about myself and my faith. On the pages that follow, I'll share stories of some of the events of that year. I promise, all these stories are true, and I hope you'll feel free to laugh with me. I love and cherish these memories—even though some of them are quite embarrassing! I've learned that in times of joy and laughter such as these, as well as in times of pain and dread, there is a deep sense of community that emerges as a gift if we are open to receiving it. The gift of community leads to an open heart and a freedom to laugh at life when it surprises us with a hiccup or dancing turkeys.

As you read these stories, I hope you'll realize that you, too, are a queen in your own way. Perhaps it's time for you to start feeling the weight of your tiara, and the freedom that comes when you realize you don't have to live and dream on your own.

AND THE WINNER IS...

In the opening scene of the film *Little Miss Sunshine,* we see a little girl, Olive, watching a beauty pageant on TV. She rewinds and watches her tape of the final moments of the Miss America pageant over and over, focusing on the response of the newly-crowned queen. As Olive watches, she mimics the queen's motions, imagining herself walking down the runway with the crowd cheering and tears pouring down her cheeks. "I want to be that girl," her actions seem to say.

I still get totally wrapped up in watching such pageants and contests on television. One recent show that played on the "pageant" idea was *America's Next Top Model.* The show was on Wednesday nights, and each week before our senior-high Bible study the girls in my youth group would sit crouched in front of the TV, watching intently as another wannabe model was cut from the competition. Each of us had a different opinion about who should win. Every week I would find the girls arriving for Bible study early so they could watch the end of the show. It's so easy to be tranquilized by the quest for beauty, for personality, and for perfection. I must admit that I'm intrigued by Tyra Banks and her entourage. In fact, I have to confess that I even checked the rules of the show last year to see what the age limit was for entering the contest. I am in a different stage of my life than most of the girls competing, yet there was still that small longing to be that model, to be Tyra's model.

That quest for beauty and confidence, for something that gives us meaning beyond what our parents have told us, never really leaves us. We look for affirmation from multiple places. Olive reminds me of the little girl in each of us, no matter how pretty or awkward we might be. She represents a beauty that is more than charm and a great figure. It's a beauty that springs from the self-confidence she had—because her grandpa told her how beautiful and great she was.

We also have this kind of relationship. God, our Creator, has made each of us with great worth and beauty. It's up to us to hold onto that truth with everything we have in us. This knowledge of a God who created us with beauty and grace can give us confidence when the world tells us we aren't beautiful, valuable, or special. Jesus once said, "If you belonged to the world, it would love you as its own. As it is, you do not belong to the world, but I have chosen you out of the world" (John 15:19).

God has made you beautiful, with unique gifts and abilities. And Jesus has chosen you as his own. The apostle Paul says it a little differently, describing each of us as "a letter from Christ...written not with ink but with the Spirit of the living God, not on tablets of stone but on tablets of human hearts. Such confidence we have through Christ before God" (2 Corinthian 3:3-4).

A unique child of God, created with worth and beauty. A person chosen by Christ, and belonging to him. A love letter from God's own Spirit. That's who you are.

YOUR CONFESSIONS

Have you ever been addicted to a reality TV show that glamorized outer perfection?

What's the difference between inner and outer beauty? Is it the same for everyone?

Think of the time you spend getting ready for school or to go out with your friends. What things could change if we spent as much time preparing the inside (spiritually, emotionally, mentally) as we did preparing the outside?

What's your biggest hang-up about your appearance?

How can you keep God at the center of your self-understanding? At the center of your dreaming?

PARADES

CONFESSION: I ONCE OPENED FOR A COUNTRY BAND AT A FESTIVAL IN NORTHERN OHIO BY DANCING THE MACARENA IN A FORMAL GOWN WITH OTHER FESTIVAL QUEENS.

I ASSURE YOU, NO SMALL CHILDREN OR ANIMALS WERE HARMED, BUT I THINK A FEW YOUNG PEOPLE MAY HAVE BEEN SCARRED FOR LIFE BY WHAT THEY WITNESSED.

SWEET CAR!

I spent my year as Miss Parade of the Hills attending local festivals all over the state of Ohio. Nearly every festival included a ride through the streets of the local town as part of the festival parade.

My parade vehicle always stood out in a crowd. It was a beauty that only certain highly safety-conscious people could really appreciate. Slick, smooth, subtle...this car was my ride in a few dozen parades that year. Most of the other festival queens had Mustangs or Cameros, usually white or another hot color. But none could compare with Miss Parade of the Hills, who sat atop a majestic beautiful beige lady. (I'm not sure whether it was a Grand Marquis or a Crown Victoria—but both are big and boisterous in the same way.) If you are not familiar with these cars, imagine a Carnival cruise ship on wheels. The front juts out quite a few feet longer than the average car. The  top (not convertible) is square and boxy—providing plenty of room for the passengers inside. The back is nearly as long as the front, and the whole car rides low—again, allowing the car to float like a luxury ocean liner.

I remember the day my chaperones, Nyoka and Linda, arrived at my house to pick me up for the first of many weekend festivals. (I'd soon grow accustomed to their weekly arrival to take me to some parade in Who-Knows-Where, Ohio.) I climbed into the illustrious big car wearing my volleyball warm ups and carrying a pillow, a hat box (holding my crown), and a shiny sequined dress on a hanger. As we pulled away from my home, they let me know we were going to Milan. I had no idea where Milan was (I was pretty sure we weren't going to Italy!) and wasn't sure about the festival queen parade thing anyway, so I just went to sleep. The car floated along, and I stayed in dreamland all the way to Milan. This nap on the way to my first festival gave me a new appreciation for big cars. Sleeping soundly in the back of a sports car or convertible has never been something I've been able to do, so I was grateful for the smooth ride of my big beige lady.

When we arrived, I hopped out of the wagon and into my formal attire. I ate with the other festival queens—all strangers, all wonderful and nice, and all with beautiful cars to sit in—emphasis on "in". As the parade approached, I couldn't stop thinking about how I was going to get on top of our big car. Did they have a ladder in the trunk? One of my chaperones helped relieve my curiosity when she opened the trunk and pulled out a welcome mat and a hand-knitted afghan (also beige). The welcome mat came equipped with rubber skid-proof backing, and for a second I wondered if they were overly protective of the beige finish on the car and expecting me to wipe off my princess feet before ascending to its roof.

Wrong again. The mat was for the front of the car, where I would be sitting. My chaperone tossed the mat on the car, patted the hood (bringing a nice metallic ringing sound to my ears), and said, "Hop up." Once I was on the car, they helped me "scoot" back so I wasn't on the very front edge of the car.

Now, if this car were a surfboard, it would have been in the long board family—so the scoot was not short or easy. It was a complex maneuver that required a lot of attention to shoes, hosiery, crown, dress, and bracelet. But eventually I made it onto the car successfully, and we drove forward to take our place in the parade. The car was so big it lurched forward like a German shepherd eager to run from its owner, only to get jolted back by a tug on its leash. I held on, feeling like I might spring forward, but the welcome mat did its job and held me safe and secure. And even if I did slide forward a bit, the hood was plenty long enough to slow me down and allow me to extend my legs for the dismount. (I learned to appreciate my parade car after it broke down one weekend and I found myself sitting on the front of a compact car similar to a Ford Focus. The hood was short and steep and lent itself to queen launching! After that, I never complained again!)

My parade career certainly wasn't what I imagined back when I dreamt of becoming a supermodel. But these parades ended up being one of the things I cherish most about my experiences as festival queen. Each parade I rode in led to a place of celebration and friendship. We'd all like to think the routes we take in life will lead to a celebration of dreams coming true and faith lived out victoriously. But if we focus our eyes on our unfortunate circumstances or on how bumpy the path is, we may give up and jump off the car. I wish I could go back to all the times in my life when I bailed on a dream because I was afraid of the path that took me there.

Think of Jesus' parade into Jerusalem (Mark 11:1-11). When he first imagined himself entering the city as God's chosen Messiah, he probably didn't picture himself on a smelly, stubborn donkey. But it didn't matter what kind of ride Jesus had that day. What mattered was his destination, and what he was going to do there. Jesus was preparing to bring salvation to the world.

We can learn something from big beige cars and from a Savior who entered humbly into the culture. Being a vibrant, life-giving Christian involves a lot of humility. The paths we take to become more like Christ aren't always paved with honors and popularity. We all have to be willing to let Christ lead our parades and not be afraid when the paths are different from what we had imagined.

GOING PLACES

It wasn't just the car I rode on during festival parades that was different from what I'd expected. The festivals themselves often led me to experiences I'd have never have dreamed of. I try to appreciate the finer things in life—but before that year, I never would have thought that gourds, turkeys, coal, tomatoes, pumpkins, ice cream, lumberjacks, moonshine, and other similar things would ever be classified as "finer" in my mind!

I have to admit, some of the festivals I was expected to attend had names that made me wonder if I should "get sick" that weekend. I never lied about my health to my chaperones—but there were times when I wanted to. But I was often surprised by the lessons I learned when going somewhere I didn't want to go. One particular festival that celebrated the scrumptious taste of juicy bratwursts helped me see that joy can be found in the unlikeliest of places.

There were a couple of reasons I wasn't all that excited about attending the Bucyrus Bratwurst Festival. First, it was a weekend when I particularly wanted to be home to spend time with my boyfriend. Second, I wasn't really happy about the two-hour drive to the little town of Bucyrus in north-central Ohio. But I tried to make the best of it. I was friends with the Bratwurst Queen (Mary Margaret, whose festival costume was a German doll dress) so I figured I'd at least have a good time with her and my other friend, Michelle, the First Town Days Queen (her festival celebrated carousel horses).

When I arrived at the festival, we did the typical routine. I found a place to change into my dress, put on my crown, and touch up my lipgloss. Linda helped me with my chunky, blingy festival bracelet which, at that point, had almost 20 charms on it. (I received a charm for every festival I attended. It jingled like

Santa's sleigh bells when I waved in parades.) I jumped onto the hood of the car, and we headed into the parade at our big-beige-car pace. It was a short parade that ended at a covered tent. It was under that tent that I found a joy I'd never experienced before—polka dancing.

I would have been more than happy to spend the evening sitting on the sidelines munching on a fat brat while others danced. But an 80-year-old man plucked me from my queenly position and pulled me onto the makeshift dance floor. He was confident and happy, which gave me a new reason to smile. I had no clue how to dance the polka, but this man didn't judge. He just smiled and led the way.

You'll never be able to dance the polka if you take yourself too seriously (especially if you've never danced the polka before). I really had no idea how to polka—but he danced and gently guided me along as I did something similar to what a two-year-old might do when listening to Congo drums or Tiki birds. I doubt we'd have won on *Dancing with the Stars*, but I enjoyed each moment to the fullest.

When I'd awakened that morning, I never could have imagined I'd be doing the polka in Bucyrus. I was thinking about how much I'd miss my boyfriend. But this random and strangely beautiful moment showed me God could be found anywhere—if we're paying attention to the gifts these moments can bring. Even the times we dread or would rather avoid can teach us something. I'll never forget this special day with friends who celebrated brats, polka dancing, and queens who had no earthly right being on the dance floor. This is where dreams come to life—in our everyday circumstances.

God has a sense of humor and, if we will let him show us the world, instead of dreading life's random, unknown, or seemingly unwanted events, we may just learn how to have joy—or at least how to dance the polka.

YOUR CONFESSIONS

Write down some everyday joys you tend to take for granted.

Talk about a really bad day that turned out great because of something unexpected.

Do you have a goal or dream that sits in your heart untouched because the path to get there seems too intimidating?

Have you ever danced the polka before? If not, give it a try! (http://www.centralhome.com/ballroomcountry/polka_steps.htm)

PLATFORM

CONFESSION: I AM A PASSIONATE PERSON ~~AND~~ WHEN I'M PASSIONATE ABOUT SOMETHING, I WANT TO SHARE IT WITH OTHERS. IN MIDDLE SCHOOL I WANTED TO SAVE THE WHALES, AND I BELIEVED EVERYONE ELSE SHOULD WANT TO SAVE THEM, TOO. WHEN I FIND A DRINK I LOVE, I TELL EVERYONE HOW AMAZING IT IS AND INSIST THAT THEY TRY IT, TOO. (7-ELEVEN SLURPEES ARE AMAZING!) I THINK IT'S IMPORTANT TO CHEW LOTS OF GUM AND HANG OUT WITH PEOPLE YOU LOVE. I THINK WOMEN SHOULD HAVE EQUAL OPPORTUNITIES IN THE CHURCH AND IN OUR WORLD. I'M PASSIONATE ABOUT HELPING THOSE WHO ARE OPPRESSED AND USE CURRICULUM LIKE THE JUSTICE MISSION AND 30 HOUR FAMINE MATERIALS IN MY YOUTH

GROUP. I THINK EVERYONE SHOULD WEAR CLOTHES MADE BY SOCIALLY-MINDED COMPANIES. (MY PERSONAL FAVORITE: WWW.JEDIDIAHUSA.COM.) I SUPPORT FRIENDS WHO HAVE THE COURAGE TO START THEIR OWN BUSINESSES.

WHEN I BELIEVE IN SOMETHING, I SHARE IT WITH THE WORLD. I GUESS YOU COULD CALL ME A PLATFORM JUNKIE.

One of the many joys of being a festival queen is having the opportunity to share your platform. Now when I say "platform," I'm not talking about the stage that contestants stand on during the pageant. I'm referring to the things you stand *for*, what you represent, the views you want to share with the community when given the chance.

I found out that being a festival queen was far more than dressing up and waving in a parade. It's also about representing your town and festival. My family loves the town of Nelsonville very much, and their love for the town gave inspiration to my long weekends on the road to the next festival. To my new queen friends and to the people who heard my speech at festivals all over Ohio that year, I represented Nelsonville and the Parade of the Hills.

My platform as Miss Parade of the Hills consisted of a quick speech I would share at each festival I attended. Some time during each weekend, all the queens would line up on stage and "sell" their various festivals. My speech changed from week to week, but the basics were pretty much the same each time. It went something like this...

> "Hello, my name is Brooklyn Alvis, 1996-1997 Miss Parade of the Hills. The Parade of the Hills is held annually the third week of August every year on Nelsonville's public square. Our festival includes local artists, an old-time fiddlers' contest, a 5K run, and the queen's competition. The week ends with a parade and plenty of food, fun, and friendship for everyone. Whether you're young, old, or somewhere in between, the Parade of the Hills seeks to bring families together, encourage community cooperation, and celebrate music, arts, and our fine Appalachian history. So head down Route 33 and join us this year at the Parade of the Hills! Thank you, and we hope to see you this August."

At first, this speech didn't mean a whole lot to me. But over time, after seeing the ways being a festival queen had brought me new friends and a better understanding of other people, I began to really believe what I was saying. The Parade of the Hills will never make national headlines. But it brings families and friends together to celebrate some of the things that matter most. I was proud to be Miss Parade of the Hills because the people who chose me believed I represented the values and beauty they hoped to see emulated in their festival. It was an honor to be chosen as festival queen in the town where many members of my family grew up and still live today. So over time, I felt more and more enthusiasm for my platform of sharing the hopes of our festival and offering an open invitation for all to come to Nelsonville and experience a week where everyone comes together as one.

Whether we've won a festival competition or not, we all have a platform. We all have to decide what we want to represent, what's important for us to share with the world. Although I am no longer Miss Parade of the Hills, I still have a platform as a follower of Christ that's been pretty consistent throughout my life.

First, I know I am saved by God's grace. I am forever thankful for God's forgiveness and for Christ's love and compassion for me and every soul who seeks it.

Second, I believe the Holy Spirit guides and protects us even during our darkest moments.

The third key point in my personal platform is the belief that God has created every one of us with unique and special gifts. There's no other person in the entire world who has the exact combination of gifts you have. I like to tell my students that if they don't share their unique gifts, passions, and strengths with the world, then no one else can. The same is true for you. No one else has what you have to offer. If you don't share those gifts, you are robbing the world of an opportunity to see part of God's image that no other person can reveal. This makes you unique. This makes you rare and highly valuable.

You reveal a piece of God's likeness that no one else shares. To deny the person you are in Christ is to hide something valuable and wonderful. Trusting that God has made you for a specific purpose can give you confidence when you feel like you have no purpose. You are beloved.

Trouble seems to camp out in our backyards in the form of doubts, low self-esteem, relationship problems, family dysfunction, heartbreak, schoolwork, and peer pressure. But when we learn to dwell in the house of God, we prevent trouble from creeping into the houses of our hearts.

Nothing can separate you from the love that keeps you seeking truth. Nothing can stand in the way of you sharing your life with the world. It is our ministry to one another to reveal God's character, to participate in God's love.

WHAT'S YOUR PLATFORM?

Each of us must decide what we stand for. What we say and do in life reflects who we are deep inside, and maybe more importantly *whose* we are. If God's fruit and God's nature dwells deep, that's what is going to come forth in our actions and in our speech.

Mother Teresa had a platform of love. She spent her life caring for those who were lost and lonely. Her book, *In the Heart of the World* (MJF Books, 1997), includes a prayer that reflects the spirit of her work: "Shine through me, and be in me, so that every soul I come in contact with may feel your presence in my soul. Let them look up and see no longer me, but only you, O Lord!"

Rahab had a platform of faith. In the book of Joshua, we learn that Rahab had been living a life of sin as a prostitute. But she realized her need for redemption and hid Israelite spies who were being pursued by the King of Jericho (Joshua 2:1-21). She did not let her past or her pride get in the way of her belief in God.

Learning was central to the platform of Jesus' friend Mary. When Jesus visited the house of sisters Mary and Martha, Mary sat at Jesus' feet, setting her heart on every word that came from his mouth (Luke 10:38-42). Her sister, Martha, scurried around the house cleaning up, jealous that Mary was getting to spend time with Jesus and angry that she wasn't helping out. Mary's platform was to be a learner; Martha's was to be a pleaser. Each of them chose what she would be about that day when Jesus came to their home.

Bethany Hamilton's platform is focused on God's saving love. In 2003, at the age of 13, Bethany was attacked by a 14-foot tiger shark while surfing in Hawaii. Bethany lost her arm in the attack but chose to resume her professional surfing career and use this tragic experience as a platform to share what God had done in her life. Her deep and abiding faith became a catalyst for sharing the good news of Christ and the hope that is available even in the worst circumstances. Bethany's life is a speech testifying to the power of God's love.

We could list many other examples, the greatest of these being Christ, who never gave up his platform of love and forgiveness. His dream comes true every time one of his children turns to him for forgiveness and decides to live out the calling given to each of them.

Even if you never give a speech in a microphone, your life speaks to the world each day. What does your life say about what is most important to you? What message do people hear when they listen to the platform of your life?

YOUR CONFESSIONS

Have you felt afraid to share with a friend about something you believed strongly?

What is unique about you? Could this uniqueness lead to a platform that could be used by God?

Would your friends say you have a platform? If other were to look at the things you value in your life, how might they describe your platform? Try to be as honest as possible.

PEOPLE

CONFESSION: SOMETIMES I LISTEN TO THE WRONG LITTLE VOICE IN MY EAR AND ACT AS IF THINGS ARE MORE IMPORTANT THAN PEOPLE. FOR EXAMPLE, WHEN I WAS FACED WITH CHOOSING BETWEEN RESPECTING MY SISTER'S PRIVACY (BY STAYING OUT OF HER ROOM) AND LOOKING GOOD (BY SNEAKING IN AND "BORROWING" HER CLOTHES TO WEAR TO SCHOOL), THERE WERE TOO MANY TIMES WHEN I DECIDED TO STEAL HER STUFF. (BETSY, I'M SORRY. IT'S BEEN TEN YEARS SINCE I SNUCK INTO YOUR ROOM AND STOLE YOUR GOOD SOCKS. I STILL HAVE THEM IF YOU WANT THEM BACK.)

Becoming a festival queen and having my weekends scheduled for me didn't always help me develop relationships with guys. However, in the same breath, I'd also say that becoming a festival queen and having my weekends scheduled for me was probably the best resource I had for developing relationships with guys.

Let me explain.

During the "let me read every book I can get my hands on" phase I went through in sixth grade, I paid little attention to guys—and cared even less whether they paid attention to me. I was content cracking up with my friend Karen in health class when our teacher talked about rationing potato chips in Ziploc bags to help with "portion control." (We could seriously devour an entire bag of Doritos in 20 minutes, about the time it took to set up a game of Monopoly.) Passing boys in the hallway was no big deal. I didn't notice them much and they didn't notice me.

It wasn't until seventh grade when I started hanging out with a girl a year older than me that I began scoping out who was cute, who was "hot," who was cool, and who I wished would notice me. Soon enough an eighth-grade guy began to notice me. His best friend was dating my older friend, and we started passing notes. Eventually one note included the question that most middle-school relationships hinge upon, "Will you be my boyfriend/girlfriend?" I don't remember who asked who. I just remember that series of notes being passed through a network of lockers and friends from the seventh-grade floor to the eighth-grade floor.

The unfortunate thing about this first romantic relationship was that my skills and experience were no match for this young man's. Let's just say if we were playing Guitar Hero on a PS2, he was playing the game at expert level and scoring in the 90th percentile, and I was playing at the beginner's level (maybe even in a practice round), operating at about 30 percent. I had too much to learn, I was naïve and inexperienced. The physical game wasn't there, and I guess this was disappointing for him. The relationship ended fairly quickly, and I felt the challenge to become a better date (at least by eighth-grade standards). It didn't take long for me to get involved with other guys. Every day I became more and more consumed with the status of my relationships with the opposite sex.

This kind of obsession can lead to really lousy decision-making. Have you ever been so consumed with a desire to succeed at something that you forgot the value of the people involved? It's like having a goal to raise money for a good cause, but being so caught up in the challenge that you steal from someone to meet your good goal. Relationships with guys are a good thing—but it's easy for us to find ourselves sacrificing things that are important to get ahead relationally.

Becoming a festival queen helped me see how important it is to have balance in my life. Wanting to have a boyfriend, or even having one, wasn't a bad thing. But I had to be careful how much of my day was consumed with me and what I wanted, and how much of my day was dedicated to serving others. It's what we do with our time and the attitude of our hearts that really matters.

THOUGHTS FOR THE RELATIONSHIP ROAD...

So I learned a few things during this vulnerable relationship-seeking time in my life that I want to share with you. This isn't an all-inclusive list, and there's no particular order to the items. They are just ideas that I hope will help you start thinking about what you have to offer the world. As you read these thoughts,

I hope you'll see glimpses of some of your own struggles and know that you aren't alone. School years can be tough—but you can do something about loving people more than you love yourself:

1. Never let a guy make you feel bad about having high standards of purity. If a guy can't understand that your physical boundaries are a way of being respectful toward him, yourself, and God, then he probably isn't someone you should consider dating.

2. Protect your female relationships. Don't let any one guy take up all your time. Boyfriends can be around one day and gone the next. Neglecting your important girl friendships could leave you without vital support when you really need it.

3. Stand for your beliefs by being a visible example of faith. If God has changed your life, let it be known by the way you live. If you put your relationship with Christ into the closet for safekeeping, away from judgment and prying eyes, you limit the power it can have to help you remain pure and honest in your relationships.

4. Tell the truth. Be honest about your life choices, especially with those who are given the great responsibility of caring for you (parents, guardians, friends). Try to communicate the details of your days (where you are going, whom you are going with, and what you might be doing). By setting up safety nets for yourself, you'll be less likely to end up doing things you'll regret later. It may sound like a jail sentence to be open with the parental units about your plans, but it serves a couple of good purposes. First, you'll have

accountability. If you tell someone what you'll be up to, you'll be less tempted to change your plans and do something you'll wish you hadn't. Second, if you are unable to see a potentially compromising or dangerous situation, you'll have someone to help you see it beforehand.

5. Take care of your mind, body, and spirit. We're constantly besieged by unrealistic images of perfection before us in magazines and on the red carpet that keep us judging ourselves and one another. If we focus too much on our bodies or outward appearance we tend to neglect the development of our mind and spirit. If we have faith in God but don't apply that faith to our daily lives, our minds and even our bodies could suffer for it. Always remember that your worth is not wrapped up in your outward appearance. Your worth is found in God who works on the inside. God's work inside us translates to an outer beauty that's worth much more than anything the world has to offer.

6. Guard your heart and try to avoid getting into a serious romantic relationship too soon. Love can lead to a physical and emotional intimacy that can be hard for a young person to balance. Unless you think the guy is fit for marriage (and you're ready for the prospect of marriage), keep it simple and fun. Enjoy the things you can do to serve others.

7. Love the "you" God created. Avoid the tendency to change yourself when everyone else does. It's like enhancing your bra with extra padding or wearing the micro-mini skirt even when you're not comfortable in it—sometimes you can be tempted to do it just because your friends are doing it. Know how beautiful

you are and be confident that God didn't make a mistake with you.

8. Focus on good health and wellness rather than focusing on your weight. I understand that this can be an ultra-sensitive topic. In college I exercised a lot (which is good) but it turned into an obsession with the size of my jeans and the number on the scale in the girls' locker room (which is not good). Losing a few extra pounds seems promising, a simple way to feel better, and to be more happy, but it often leads to more emptiness. The times in my life when I've enjoyed recreation for fun (rather than burning off pounds) and have been mindful of what I ate because of its nutritional value rather than its lack of calories, I've felt better and less under pressure. The struggle may still exist, but I've learned how to cope in positive ways, which really helps my self-image (in the light of God instead of in the light of Hollywood), which helps my relationships.

9. Risk being a dork in front of people (including guys). You'll be a breath of fresh air in a world full of people who are often scared to show their true colors. Confident girls are attractive because they aren't hiding anything. You may even inspire other girls to be confident in their weird and quirky sides. God made you just right—rejoice in it! (Even if your identity is more "Ugly Betty" than Scarlett Johansson, rejoice!)

10. Love the people around you. Even when you are treated harshly or judged by others, choose love by not returning the favor. Be a woman of grace and goodness. Someone who will respect you, honor your beliefs, and love you back will come along eventually.

WASTED TIME

If I could take back all of the time I've wasted vying for the attention of some guy, I'd probably have a few extra weeks or months to learn and grow in other ways. This is where being a festival queen drastically changed my view of relationships. It helped me see I was obsessed with something that would never fulfill me. Gaining daily acceptance from guys didn't need to be the most important thing in my life. Over time, doing things for others and becoming more knowledgeable about the person I was becoming took the place of my constant need for male affirmation.

When I won the title of Miss Parade of the Hills, I was dating a nice young man from a town about 20 minutes from mine. I met him over the summer at a church camp. He was good looking, athletic, had lots of friends, and—best of all—he was a Christian. We started dating even though we couldn't see each other that often. We'd talk on the weekends or meet for a movie or dinner once a week. It was a change for me, since I was used to having a boyfriend around me every day. (Up until that point, I'd had a steady boyfriend since the eighth grade.) Still, we were content with how things were going. We both wished we could see each other more, but we were okay with the circumstances. We continued to grow in our personal faith and in our relationship, and the distance was helping each of us develop as individuals.

Then I won the pageant.

Weekends had been the only times I was able to see my boyfriend—and suddenly they were all taken away. I dreaded seeing the calendar that marked the weekends I would be frolicking in the hills of Ohio promoting our festival. It seemed like such a waste at first, and I was heartbroken to know that my boyfriend would be doing other things and hanging out with other people when I was traveling.

The first festival was sort of frightening. It was the Milan Melon Festival. We celebrated melons. We ate melons. A melon queen was crowned, and melon crafts were sold in tents. At the time, it seemed like life couldn't get any more random and unfair! What I see now that I didn't see then is that I would become a better person through experiences like these. The Melon Queen would become a good friend of mine. I would grow to love crazy festivals and crazy people, because in each person is a shimmering reflection of our creative God.

As much as I missed my boyfriend during all those weekends, I was blessed to be able to focus on loving others and accepting others in their own worlds and ways of living. If I had spent every spare moment with my boyfriend, I'd have missed out on a great opportunity to see the value of community and of learning to cherish even the most random moments that come our way.

How many people do you know who've had the chance to sit on top of the world's largest pumpkin? Have you ever met someone with a recipe for moonshine? Have you ever eaten a funnel cake and a side of fried rice next to a carousel of horses in an evening gown?

I've shared some really rich moments with people I would have never met if I'd stayed focused on myself and what I thought I wanted. Through those experiences I learned that God sometimes opens doors in the most random and unpredictable ways. These doors often lead us to a choice...

We have the choice to seize the day as an opportunity to love others, or to be depressed in our circumstances. I could have let that crown and the obligations that went with it make me miserable. But somehow by the grace of God I was open to what it might bring me. And it brought me to a place where I could love other people more than I loved myself—a lesson that takes a lifetime for each of us to learn, but one that's worth the effort.

As for my boyfriend, we found ways to stay in touch and ended up sharing a great senior year together, festivals and all! He respected my commitments, and I respected his. When I spent weekends traveling, he spent his weekends playing basketball and doing other things. We went to youth group and to the occasional movie together, but our days weren't consumed with each other. It was a respect and a trust that benefited both of us in high school. And it helped us build a strong relationship—we've been married for nine years now! I'm thankful for the days we spent time learning who we were in Christ as individuals before we dedicated ourselves to each other.

WITH WONDER AND AWE

I remember sitting on top of my big car during one parade, looking out at the kids lining the streets, and thinking, *These little kids actually think I'm a queen!* My charm bracelet jingled as I waved to each little boy and girl. They looked back at me with eyes full of wonder, awe, and hope. They couldn't care less what kind of car I was riding on. They saw a crown and knew I was a queen.

It's the same way with you, wherever you are. Your circumstances may not be the greatest. But every day you have the opportunity to show love to those around you. But when people see the fruits of your life, they will know you are a daughter of the Most High. They will know you are someone they can trust and respect and stand in awe of.

I'll never forget how little girls looked at me during parades all over the state of Ohio. They stared wide-eyed at my crown, hoping someday to have one of their own. If I'd let my personal schedule get in the way, I wouldn't have these sweet memories of childhood wonder. I learned something on the parade route. If I had skipped the parade, I would have missed the blessing. I represented something special to others even when I didn't recognize it. We must realize the beauty we all have to share.

You are what you represent.

The fruits that come from your life identify you as one sent from God, sent with a dream and an identity the world needs. Other people are important and worthy of our time and love.

And, God wants to teach us something, in the little moments—even on big cars in melon and bratwurst parades.

YOUR CONFESSIONS

What kinds of things distract you from strengthening your relationship with God and going after your dreams wholeheartedly?

Have you ever been so consumed with something that you forgot to take care of other important things? What would help you have more balance?

Think about the things that might get too big in your life. (Possibilities might include school, clothes, guys, dating, sports, etc.) How do these things distract you from growing in God? What things should you be most careful about keeping in good balance? In other words, where are you weak?

Psalm 46:1 says, "God is our refuge and strength, an ever-present help in trouble." How can you learn to trust God with your relationships?

PRESENTS

CONFESSION: I ONCE "RE-GIFTED" A PRESENT I'D BEEN GIVEN WITHOUT REALIZING THE TAG FROM THE ORIGINAL GIVER WAS STILL TAPED ON THE BOTTOM. OOPS!

There is a longstanding tradition of gift-giving in the festival queen world. Each time I went to a festival, there was a luncheon for all the queens in attendance. At all these luncheons, the outgoing queen of that festival (who was about to end her reign with the crowning of a new queen) would give presents to all the attending queens. The presents were tokens of love and appreciation, and they were selected to represent the queen who bestowed them. When I was queen and traveling every weekend, I would bring a new gift home at the end of each weekend and place it in my cedar chest.

I still use some of these gifts today. At the Gourd Festival I received a painted Santa Claus (made out of a hollowed-out gourd, of course). I still use this gourd Santa to top my Christmas tree every year. It's probably the most random tree-topper in the world, and it wasn't meant for that purpose, but every year I pull out my gourd Santa and remember that very special year of friends. There were other gifts—pins and buttons, pictures and frames, recipes for moonshine and bricks of clay. No matter how peculiar or beautiful a gift, each one reminds me of a person, a place, and a very special time that taught me more than I ever would have expected.

When it was my time to present a gift to my queen friends, I purchased a bunch of glass Mason jars from the dollar store. I filled them all up with Starburst jellybeans and put a blue gingham topper on each one. The jellybeans had no correlation with my festival (since I was "Miss Parade of the Hills"), but they signified a sweetness that each girl represented to me, and the assortment of different flavors, gifts, and talents that were represented in our group.

I learned something really cool from these festival queen gifts. Each girl gave something unique. Each present fit the taste, personality, or festival theme of the girl who gave it. I could never give a gourd away at my festival, because I didn't live in Mt. Gilead where the Gourd Show is. I couldn't give ice cream, because the Utica Ice Cream Queen had that taken care of. And I could never offer the polka like the queen at the Bucyrus Bratwurst Festival. But through the gifts and graces of many loving queens I came to understand the importance of diversity and of each individual's God-given characteristics, strengths, and personalities.

Every one of us has a present to offer the world when we are true to our faith in God, true to ourselves, and steadfast in going after our dreams. Each of us is made from a special recipe no one else can duplicate. We are all fearfully, wonderfully, and uniquely made. (See Psalm 139:14.)

You are the only person who can give what you have to offer. God has provided each of us with unique gifts to share with others. Learning to accept and embrace my own gifts has been one of the best things that's ever happened to me. I don't have to pretend to be someone else. I am free to be me.

A RECIPE

Take one part David and one part Kelly, mix in a bit of Twyla, Bill, James, Virginia, and a pinch from the great-greats. Fold in one fine man, Coy (and his relatives, too).

Shake together half cups of Nelsonville, Fort Myers, Newark, Lancaster, Elmhurst, Mount Vernon, Orlando, Rockledge, and Southlake.

Sift in remnants of trailers, apartments, and townhouses.

Mix with six siblings and various pets (some dead, some missing) for added flavor.

Add parts from the beach, the city, and a little restaurant called "Down the Hatch."

Season with too much MTV and lots of Nickelodeon reruns.

Throw in dashes of middleschool love and

HIGHSCHOOL BASKETBALL GAMES.

ADD IN "SAVE THE WHALES," CLAIRE'S BOUTIQUE, AND A TELEPHONE IN MY OWN ROOM.

SPRINKLE IN PORTIONS OF FESTIVAL QUEENS, SCHOOL CHEERLEADERS, AND DRAMAS ON THE STAGE.

STIR IN PIECES OF A YOUTH PASTOR (ROB), A MENTOR (RICK), A POET (EDWINA), A WRITER (ANNE), A DREAMER (MIKE), AND SOME REALLY GREAT FRIENDS (LINDSAY, JEN, AND HOLLY).

POUR IN A SAMPLING OF GIRL FREAK-OUT PARTIES (PREFERABLY AT CAMP), SECRETS, AND THINGS WE DON'T TALK ABOUT ON PAPER.

MIX IN ONE CHURCH (DON'T MIND THE LUMPINESS OR THE VARYING COLORS AND PERSONALITIES).

ALLOW FOR AS MUCH JESUS AS CAN FIT IN THE POT. (REMOVE OTHER THINGS TO MAKE ROOM IF NECESSARY...IT WILL PROBABLY BE NECESSARY.)

ADD IN COMPASSION AND JUSTICE (SUBSTITUTE FORGIVENESS WHEN COMPASSION AND JUSTICE AREN'T AVAILABLE).

GATHER LESSONS LEARNED, MISTAKES MADE, AND AN ABUNDANCE OF GOD'S GRACE.

MIX ALL THINGS TOGETHER AND SERVE WITH A SIDE OF LOVE.

From this recipe, I hope you can see how different I am from anyone else. God only made one me. While others may share some similar traits, no one can duplicate my past, my memories, my upbringing, and my personality. In the same way, there is only one you. You have something unique to offer the world.

How you share your gifts as you journey through this world matters more than you know. The New Testament repeats this message: All of us have gifts to offer that will bless our world if we are willing to share them. God has gifted each of us with a unique calling, and we shouldn't neglect it. We shouldn't let our gifts fade away.

My mom spent a lot of money on private violin lessons for me. She sacrificed quite a bit to support me and help me improve. Because of her good investment, I ended up with the gift of being able to play the violin.

But if our gifts are left on the shelf too long, they can get rusty and out of shape. When I entered high school I spent my time on lots of things—but practicing the violin wasn't one of them. When I regained my interest and returned to the violin, it was harder to play because I'd let my skills sit dormant for too long. All the time, money, and energy spent on making me a better violinist was awesome—but for it to be a blessing to others, I needed to keep practicing and using the gift.

I haven't touched a violin in years. To this day, my husband still hasn't heard me play. It's not because I can't remember how to play. I still remember where to place my fingers, and I'm sure I could muster up a great rendition of "Mary Had a Little Lamb"! It's because I'm ashamed. I've left the gift sitting for so long that I don't know how to use it anymore. I'm also afraid to try, because I know that getting the gift back into shape will take time, hard work, and dedication—and my fingers just might get sore!

Isn't this how we are with the gifts God has given to us? Yes, there are times when using our gifts might seem easy and will fit seamlessly into our everyday lives. But what do you do when they don't seem to fit anymore or we lose interest? What do we do when our attention gets diverted unknowingly and our gifts get a little rusty?

Our lives are meant to be a gift to those around us and a gift to the God who created us. Romans 12:1-2 says:

> *Therefore, I urge you, brothers and sisters, in view of God's mercy, to offer your bodies as a living sacrifice, holy and pleasing to God—this is true worship. Do not conform to the pattern of this world, but be transformed by the renewing of your mind. Then you will be able to test and approve what God's will is—his good, pleasing and perfect will.*

The God who created us and gave us all we have invites us to offer ourselves back as a living gift. This is true worship. This is the key to understanding God's will for all of us.

RE-GIFT...IT'S OKAY!

"Re-gifting" is one of those things people laugh about and rarely admit to, but secretly most of us know we've done it before. You get a nice gift, but it really isn't your style or taste, or maybe you have something similar already. And then one day, after you've forgotten to buy a gift for a party, you decide this gift you received is worthy of being passed on to someone else.

But there are some critical unspoken re-gifting rules. For example, one shall never re-gift at a party or dinner that the original giver will be attending. Another rule: Make sure all gift cards from the original giver are replaced with new ones *before* the gift is given again. These are just a few words of advice from someone who knows firsthand the risks involved with re-gifting.

Perhaps you find the idea of re-gifting totally appalling and rude. If so, I hope you can forgive my next statement: *It is essential to your spiritual growth and your relationship with Christ to re-gift on a daily basis.*

That's right—God wants you to wrap up that gift you have in your possession and give it away! I'm not talking about the Captain Jack Sparrow journal you got from your aunt on your last birthday. I'm talking about the innate gifts God has given to you. You have to give them away. You need to share them with the world. The world is waiting for you to take what's been given to you by a loving Giver (God) and pass it on. No one else can offer what you have been given, and no one else will receive the blessing unless you are willing.

The next time you have a funny conversation with your friends about re-gifting, smile and know that, in your own way, you re-gift everyday. It is your queenly duty to share your gifts in thanks for all you have been given.

YOUR CONFESSIONS

If you were to write a recipe for yourself, what would it say? Use the space here to write a recipe for you.

MY RECIPE

_____

_____

_____

_____

_____

_____

_____

_____

_____

Look over your recipe. Can you see the amazing person you are, and all you have to offer the world?

Track down a copy of the song "Beautiful Flower" by India Arie. Listen to the words. Do you feel beautiful, resilient, and powerful enough to change the world for good? Do you know how much God loves the "you" found in you?

A WANDERING QUEEN

CONFESSION: I'M NATURALLY PRONE TO WANDERING, AND SOMETIMES GETTING LOST. WHILE WANDERING AROUND MALLS, GROCERY STORES, LIBRARIES, MUSEUMS—OR EVEN AT A GAS-STATION MAGAZINE RACK—IT'S NOT RARE FOR ME TO LOSE TRACK OF THE PEOPLE I'M WITH BECAUSE I'VE BECOME ENAMORED WITH SOMETHING FASCINATING THEY'VE OBVIOUSLY OVERLOOKED. WANDERING CAN GET EMBARRASSING WHEN, AFTER YOU'VE LOST TRACK OF YOUR GROUP, YOU FIND YOURSELF WALKING AROUND LIKE A TWO-YEAR-OLD IN SEARCH OF HER MOMMY, LOOKING DOWN EVERY AISLE HOPING TO FIND THE PERSON YOU'VE LOST. IT'S DOUBLY HUMILIATING WHEN YOU DON'T EVEN REALIZE YOU'VE WANDERED AWAY FROM THE GROUP AND

START TALKING TO STRANGERS. I CAN'T TELL YOU HOW
MANY TIMES I'VE BEEN IN THE GREETING-CARD AISLE OF A
STORE AND HAVE READ A CARD ALOUD TO A PERFECT STRANGER
(THINKING MY SISTER, OR FRIEND, OR WHOEVER WAS STILL
STANDING NEXT TO ME). IT'S A GREAT WAY TO PROVE YOU
ARE FRIENDLY...OR MAYBE A LITTLE INSANE.

"Only an empty soul can be filled."
Edwina Gately, *I Hear a Seed Growing* (Source Books, 1990)

One summer a few years ago I was wandering in search of...
something. At the time, I thought I was looking for food. I was
at a summer camp for students in Central Florida. My role as
pastor, chaperone, leader, counselor, friend, and late-night-
girl-party-leader had left me feeling exhausted. I was tired
and hungry—and the steady diet of camp food wasn't helping
matters. There are only so many times you can eat hamburgers
on Monday (the kind that magically turn into "Salisbury steak"
on Tuesday and "shepherd's pie" on Wednesday). The entrees
taste pretty good for a day or two. But eventually folks begin
to discover that the croutons on the salad bar make a really
good meal when combined with heaps of ranch dressing and
shredded cheese. (Later in the week you might try adding bacon
bits and club crackers for variety.) There's always the cereal bar
as a last resort for dinner—until the Fruit Loops run out (usually
by the second day of camp) and everyone is left with tasty bran
flakes.

So camp food isn't the greatest. But who ever said it
would be? I've learned to embrace the fact that camp food is
only meant to sustain us for the time we are at camp. It's simply

meant to give us enough calories to burn for the next shaving cream fight or three-on-three basketball game.

I was definitely hungry that night. But I was hungry for something more than food. I was hungry for answers, hungry for hope that would lead me in helping the girls that I met at camp. I realized that most of the girls (including myself) had been wandering in the desert, burdened by society's pressure and standards to be pretty, playful, and perfect. These pressures can leave us feeling empty and alone.

In Rosalind Wiseman's book, *Queen Bees & Wannabes: Helping Your Daughter Survive Cliques, Gossip, Boyfriends, & Other Realities of Adolescence* (Three Rivers, 2002), there's a sad quote from a 15-year-old named Joni. She says, "I have never met a person who thinks she is pretty. You sit and pick apart every flaw. The combined list of how you don't measure up really adds up." I've heard this story from so many young women, and I've personally felt the burden of these words.

Much like the Israelites who wandered through the wilderness for forty years, unsure about who they were and this dream they were chasing of a Promised Land, we are also searching—sometimes in the wrong places. We find ourselves wandering in circles without a compass, and these fruitless searches can lead to the decay of our physical, emotional, and spiritual beings. So my desire that night was to seek a remedy for this great tragedy that claims the lives and souls of so many beautiful and gifted young women.

CAMP CLARITY

After a couple of years as a counselor at that camp, I'd developed great relationships with some of the girls from across Central Florida who gathered there every year. But when I was asked that year to share during the "girl talk" at the high school camp, I was forced to deal with my own wandering and confusion about my life and my future. Were these girls experiencing the same frustrations I did while growing up? Since I didn't feel equipped with many answers, did I have anything good to say to them?

I knew these girls were wrestling with many different issues and problems that summer. At the very least I wanted to open the door and help them see they were not alone. Whatever "it" was in their life, I wanted to offer them hope. But how could I help these awesome young women believe in their own goodness, when there were forces all around them (commercials, magazines, Internet, at school, in books, and on runways) that said they were not good and not special? I was in my early twenties—and still struggling to figure out what was so special about me! I had a deep desire to help other girls see their God-given goodness, because it had taken so long for me to figure it out. I wanted them to know now! Somehow I had survived adolescence and found a new identity in my relationship with God. The supermodel dreams of my youth hadn't really "come true," but God was reshaping how I thought about my dreams. I wanted each of these girls to discover an identity she could be proud and passionate about. I knew I wasn't going to be able to do all those things in a 40-minute speech, but my own wandering coupled with a hope and belief in something greater than my strength wouldn't let me put these questions aside.

LEAVING WANDERING BEHIND... DISCOVERING A LAND OF PROMISE

I believe God longs to help each of us move from that place of wandering and uncertainty into a place of purpose. God wants us to live in a land of plenty and to become strong in the Lord. Knowing that God can provide everything you need will make a difference in your life, in your struggles, and even in your dreaming.

The Israelites who wandered though the wilderness eventually made their way to God's Promised Land—a land "flowing with milk and honey" (Exodus 3:8). God wants the same good things for his children today. It's funny to think about: God offers us all the food we need, but we stay parked at the salad bar eating croutons and ranch dressing. God wants to give us the sweet fruits of life. God awaits us with a promised land full of fruit and blessing.

I've wandered so many times from the path of God's protection and care. Sometimes it's like I'm a puppy who discovers the scent of another animal and follows where it leads, sniffing around, never looking up, only to find herself on the other side of the pond with no clue how to get home. It's been those times of "sniffing" down the wrong paths that have led me to be afraid and confused about who I am and where I belong. At every stage of life, I've found myself looking for something different—for approval, for recognition and honor, for more stuff, for guys to notice me and love me, for love, for girls to love and include me, for independence, for more than words in a relationship, for whatever someone else had that I thought I lacked. And even if I was able to get what I was seeking, I discovered new feelings of discontent to replace them. These desires always led me deeper into the wilderness of unknowing and farther from the knowledge of who I truly am. But when I finally began looking for a relationship with God, my hunger for these other things lessened.

As I've said, my childhood dream was to become a supermodel. God has taken that deep longing of my heart, transformed it, and made it come true. I've become a "supermodel"—not in the way I imagined, but in ways that have brought me great joy and satisfaction. Whoever you are, God wants to give you the fruit you need to satisfy your soul. God wants to help you not only survive, but thrive in your lifetime. I discovered contentment as I searched for answers to life's questions, something that no one but God could deliver.

What is it that you are searching for?

YOUR CONFESSIONS

When was the last time you felt really lost and searching for something? What was it like?

What is it like when wandering leads to hungers that can't be satisfied? How do you usually respond?

When we fill our bodies with junk food rather than food with nutritional value, it can leave us feeling empty and even tired. The same is true spiritually. Have you ever taken the world's promises and believed them instead of listening to God's?

Think about your story and your dreams. Where do you see God at work right now? (Even if you are experiencing a difficult or painful time, aim to see where God is stretching you and strengthening your gifts.)

FAITH AND FRUIT

CONFESSION: It may seem funny, but I'm not sure whether a pumpkin is a fruit or a vegetable. (I'm leaning toward fruit.) Either way, I should tell you that I once came across some pumpkins in the trunk of my boyfriend's car (he's now my husband) a few days after Halloween. I was suspicious because just the night before, very near his house, someone had rolled quite a few pumpkins down a hill (where they all smashed at the bottom). I'm not saying Coy had anything to do with the fruit rolling. (After all, these are _MY_ confessions.) But he has never been one to make pies. . .

WONDER WOMAN, THE TOOTH FAIRY, AND BELIEVING IN THE IMPOSSIBLE

It might seem surprising at first, but believing in something we can't see actually comes to us quite naturally when we're young. Think about your own childhood. You probably believed in things your parents told you about. For example, I believed in Santa Claus, the Tooth Fairy, and the Easter Bunny as a child because I trusted the people passing down the stories. I had a childlike, believing faith. I never met Wonder Woman, Batman, Minnie Mouse, or the Care Bears, but I *knew* they existed. In fact, I loved the Care Bears so much that I believed if I thought about them long enough before going to sleep that the freaky-scary person under my bed couldn't come out to get me when I fell asleep. These are precious moments of childlike faith, when we believe in something so much that it takes away our fears.

But as we grow up, our understanding begins to sneak up on our imaginations. We feel silly talking seriously about our childhood heroes anymore. Phrases like "I remember when I used to believe in..." begin to flood into our conversations.

We also believe in real living people whom we might never actually see, meet, touch, or talk to. People who have gone before me like Mother Teresa, Princess Diana, Martin Luther King, Jr., Elvis Presley, and Mozart have all had a profound impact on the way I live my life. And that's true of others who are still living. I've never met Oprah, Bono, Gary Haughan, or Mary J. Blige, but I believe in some of the choices each of them has made, how they've lived, or particular things they have stood for. The speeches of Dr. Martin Luther King Jr.

inspire me—it's hard not to have faith when someone else's faith is so convincing. I look up to people like Princess Diana who refused to ignore the needs of others. Elvis and Mozart had vision, passion, and unmatched creativity. Gary Haughan has devoted his life to freeing girls trapped in sexual slavery. Mary J. Blige was my favorite recording artist when I was in seventh grade—and still is today. Her success and determination over the last 10 years tell us something about her character and what she believes. I want to be like that.

We all have weaknesses and experience tragedy. Even these great and inspiring people have known their share of burdens and heartache. But the good things can overshadow the bad. They can give us hope and a message to hold on.

It takes imagination and an open heart to believe in something we can't see—and that is certainly true when it comes to faith in God. The Book of Hebrews says, "Faith is being sure of what we hope for and certain of what we do not see" (Hebrews 11:1). When I was fifteen I met this unseen God and his son, Jesus, and I felt the power of the Holy Spirit. This experience changed my life—and some of my friends thought I was losing my mind. When I started living differently, certain of something I could not see, it really made me look crazy. But faith is like that. It may seem like foolishness to others, but it makes sense to those who know what it's like to experience forgiveness, joy, wholeness, and hope.

One of my first encounters with real faith was when my grandpa used to take me places in his rickety old truck. The hinges on the doors would creak, and it smelled of hard work and greasy parts. Grandpa seemed to be the person with all the answers. Questions flowed naturally when I was with him. One day, as we were riding in his truck after an Ohio thunderstorm,

I noticed a large rainbow stretching from one end of the sky to the other. "Grandpa, where do rainbows come from?"

Chewing on a handful of Tums and glancing at the sky as he drove, Grandpa told me rainbows were God's way of telling us that we should have hope and that earth won't ever be destroyed again by flood because of human sin. (If you want to read about God's rainbow covenant, check out Genesis 9:12-17.) I shared Grandpa's faith that God would honor this promise—even though I was young and unable to really understand the Bible on my own. Grandpa told me the Bible story of how Noah's family had been saved from a devastating flood. Noah believed in something he definitely couldn't see (God's promise of protection in the face of a worldwide disaster). He set his mind to building a gi-normous ark and to being faithful. Looking like a crazy delusional man didn't matter much to someone with this kind of trust and determination.

Faith comes to us naturally if we are willing to receive it. And faith requires us to be obedient, to follow wherever the Lord may lead us.

Most children find faith to be easy. The difficult part comes when we are old enough to decide what we believe and what we don't, based on our own questions. As a young teenager, I began to struggle with my faith when I didn't fit in with all of the other church kids. I would arrive at church with my grandfather and my sister. We would wear our best church dresses and get the warmest smiles and handshakes every morning as we arrived. A sweet woman named Margaret would always check off my attendance when I entered the church building. But I began to notice that there were different groups or cliques among the youth at the church. When it was time to move from children's church into Sunday school divided by grades, I lied about my age so I could be in the bigger class.

My sister was left with everyone else in children's church, and we both felt alone. The postcards I got in the mail when I was absent helped me feel loved, but they also brought feelings of guilt and sadness. The cliques at church only multiplied, and I never found a niche.

There was one Sunday school teacher, Mrs. Fender, who taught us about real life stuff, and she became my haven. Mrs. Fender taught us about things like our speech, life choices, and about loving one another. Every week we would focus on a particular Bible verse and make a craft to represent that verse. I still have a pair of lips I made with words about not letting any "unwholesome talk come from our mouths" (Ephesians 4:29). But eventually, it was time for me to change classes, and I faced the clique problem again. Slowly, my sister and I became more and more active in middle school, and my faith faded into the background. Church became a passing memory—and the further I got from church, the more convinced I was that I couldn't go back.

Although I wouldn't have said it this way then, I'd replaced faith in God with faith in other things that seemed more profitable to me. At the time I didn't see my constant need for attention as faith in anything, but I was actually placing faith in relationships I thought could fulfill my every need. I had faith in having male friends, believing that having them would make me more popular, prettier, and more fulfilled. I had faith in my girlfriends to bring me happiness and fill my social life with things that would make us the best memories. I had faith in my appearance, faith that it would get me more boys and more friends, good grades, and a ticket out of trouble. I gave up a faith in God because it didn't fit in my world where most things revolved around me, and instead adopted a faith in people and things that could never satisfy my deep and growing need for love and acceptance.

Like a fly on the canvas of a painting, we often struggle to see the big picture when we are so close to the action. All of us look back on times in our lives and wish we "knew then what we know now." Working as a youth pastor and watching girls grow up before my eyes, I see so many ways in which they are like I was—in spite of all of our differences. We all come to a point in our lives when we decide what to believe about ourselves, about our world, and about God. When we are young, it can help to listen to the voices of those who have lived before us for help as we make choices and build worldviews. Sometimes we're too close to the canvas of our immediate everyday lives to see things clearly.

I experience awe when I'm able to see part of the big picture of my life. As we examine and deconstruct our own stories, sometimes God gives us a glimpse of the bigger picture. I've noticed that, in the times when I tried to hide my faith in God in the cedar chest of my life (where it could stay safe and away from my daily activities), my faith would seek me out. My faith in God was still with me, just like the cedar chest that sits dormant in my room day after day, untouched until I have an urge to look at its contents again.

Losing faith in God is not the same as losing your faith in a boy, a friend, a celebrity, or an organization. Losing faith in these things is easy. In those situations, we can walk away, choose not to deal with that person or thing anymore, and (for the most part) allow it to sink into the recesses of our mind. Faith in God is different. It's something we can't fully understand. So it's scary. It's unpredictable. It sometimes looks different from what we'd envisioned. God never lets us go, even when we think we've locked our faith away. Couple that with the Holy Spirit's free range on the earth and in our hearts and you get a life filled with unexpected turns. But when we are connected to Jesus, who is the vine, the Spirit provides us with special skills or tools to navigate the terrain of life. These gifts are called the fruit of the Spirit.

I ♥ FRUIT

After my husband and I bought a house in Texas, we decided to plant a tree in our front yard. We didn't have a whole lot of extra money, so we bought a very small sapling, instead of one that had been growing for a few years. It was so sad looking, but we knew that someday it would be a beautiful strong magnolia tree.

Every day we would go outside to watch it grow. Have you ever tried watching a plant grow? It's like waiting for water to boil or for the light to turn green when you're running late for school. Each day we'd inspect its little branches for signs of fruit—or signs of anything! For a long time, we didn't see anything. We watered it every day, afraid the tiny tree might shrivel up and die before it was ever given a chance. Finally, we began to notice little buds growing on the ends of the branches. If we'd messed with those buds or removed them from the tree, they would never have unfolded to make leaves. Eventually, a few leaves sprouted up and new life began to shoot out. It took a long time, but when life did reach out from the earth, it was obvious that it was magnolia life. I would have really freaked out if our new magnolia tree started producing pinecones or coconuts. It was meant to produce wide and shiny magnolia leaves to shade our home.

The same thing happens in our relationship with God. When we are in communion with God through our relationship with Jesus Christ, we become connected to the Source of life. Our lives are like branches that produce the fruit of whatever we are connected to. We are responsible for the grace we have received, to respond to it and be willing to grow. We must water it and allow it to be pruned.

What are the fruits that God will grow in us? Paul tells us in the Book of Galatians, "The fruit of the Spirit is love, joy, peace, patience, kindness, goodness, faithfulness, gentleness, and self-control...since we live by the Spirit, let us keep in step with the Spirit" (Galatians 5:22, 25)

We all have the opportunity for these gifts to bud and come to life in us as we follow Jesus. These fruits of the Spirit give our lives true meaning and purpose. We don't have to wander aimlessly, searching for something to nourish our famished hearts. We simply have to ask God to give us strength to live by the Spirit today.

Are you ready to receive and respond to God's gift of fruit?

YOUR CONFESSIONS

What fictional characters did you believe in as a child? What was it about them that most intrigued you?

Whom do you believe in now? Have you met that person before? What contributes to your faith in that person?

How is belief in God an act of faith?

How will having the fruit of the Spirit help you live your dreams?

Would you say you are connected to the vine (Jesus) today? If you are, what fruit is God producing in you? What fruit do you think God wants to flourish in your life? What fruits aren't growing so well?

RUMORS

CONFESSION: I AM ALWAYS DRAWN TO THE GOSSIP MAGAZINES IN THE CHECKOUT LINE AT THE GROCERY STORE. I HAVE NO IDEA WHO MANY OF THE PEOPLE ON THE COVERS ARE—BUT FOR SOME COMPULSIVE YET UNEXPLAINABLE REASON, I SEEM TO CARE ABOUT WHETHER OR NOT THEY ARE PREGNANT, IN A FASHION DISASTER, OR IN A FIGHT WITH A FRIEND.

"Dear Jesus, help us to spread your fragrance everywhere we go."
Mother Teresa, *In the Heart of the World* (MJF Books, 1997)

CONFESSIONS OF A Not-So-SUPERMODEL

In *Queen Bees & Wannabes* (Three Rivers, 2002), author Rosalind Wiseman estimates that about 99.99 percent of girls gossip. She calls teasing and gossip "the lifeblood of cliques and popularity" for teenage girls. If that's true, then it's pretty much inevitable that you'll be the subject of gossip from time to time during your high school years—and maybe you'll even spread a rumor or two yourself.

As Christian young women, we must be aware that rumors and gossip can impact how we view ourselves, our social status, and even our spirituality. Learning how to cope with this is essential to our feeling healthy and whole. So let me tell you about some rumors I dealt with while growing up. Then I'd like to share with you some rumors that are really worth listening to. They could change your life!

Gossip makes me sad—especially when I'm the center of it. I remember one of the first times a rumor affected me deeply. I was in the fifth grade, and someone told me that my "boyfriend" Craig didn't really like the black Raiders hat I got for him. That little bit of gossip made me doubt that he liked the hat. Whether the rumor was true or not doesn't really matter at this point—we stopped being a couple when things got weird, and he gave the hat back. (You know how quickly things change at that age—you can be best buds with someone one day and calling each other names the next. We've all been there.)

Or take the time in eighth grade, when the cute guy on the baseball team supposedly liked me. We passed notes a couple of times, and then someone told me he really didn't like me. I believed the rumor and started talking to other guys. I was surprised a few months later when he asked me out. We dated for two years.

RUMORS

Rumors can and will creep into your faith and distract you from the truth if you aren't careful. They can intimidate you and keep you wondering if your dreams are worth the investment. Here's what happened to me:

I was 15 years old when I first went to youth camp for the summer. I lived in Ohio, but the camp was in Kansas—which was not only 15 hours from home, but also 15 hours from my boyfriend. Each night's worship services taught me new things about the love of Jesus and about the new creation I could become. I wasn't a horrible person, but I knew there were things in my life that needed a change. I wasn't heading down all of the best paths. I was ready for a makeover. All I needed was forgiveness—and it was right there staring at me, waiting for me to accept the invitation. When I finally did accept God's forgiveness, it led to some soul searching that changed a lot for me. I realized I'd have to make some hard decisions about my way of living.

On one of the final days of camp, after struggling with the decision all night long, I knew my boyfriend and I needed to break up. If we didn't, we'd probably end up somewhere physically that didn't honor God or each other. The following afternoon I found some time to call him. I still remember talking on the pay phone that day, breaking up with someone I loved very much. I knew it hurt him—and it hurt me, too. But it was something I needed to do to start over. And it was a good decision. I had doubts at the time about whether we needed to break up, but later experiences showed me that I did the right thing. So I don't regret the decision.

But there is one thing I do regret.

I regret how seriously I took the rumors I heard after that decision. You see, my family moved to another school district during that summer. After camp, my sister and I begged our parents to let us go to a local Christian school that some friends from church attended. Even though we'd be changing schools either way, if we went to the Christian school, we'd know some people and wouldn't have to leave our hometown.

They decided to let us go. A lot changed for us that year. For the first time we had to abide by a dress code. We weren't allowed to say words like "darn" and "gosh" because they resembled other words too closely. It was a very different culture, and a big change for all of us. (I have three younger siblings.)

All this happened right after the breakup. No one ever saw me again at our public school. But I soon began to hear that rumors were spreading at my old school, not only about why I'd broken up with my boyfriend, but also about why our family decided to transfer from a public school to a Christian school. To this day, I wish I'd had a chance to tell all of my old public school friends what happened at summer camp. I'm not sure what people really thought, but based on the rumors, I thought most of my old friends had judged me. The rumor that my sister and I had left school to become nuns hurt me. (Today I'd consider it a great honor to be compared to someone as dedicated and compassionate as a Sister of Charity! But as a young teenager it was devastating.)

I embraced my new life at a new school with new friends and a new faith. But there was something missing in it all. Where there should have been great confidence and joy, there was a void. I wanted to tell my ex-boyfriend how much I still cared about him, but that I needed time to develop as a person and as a Christian before I dedicated myself to another relationship. But the opportunity never came up. I felt bad sometimes. I felt guilty.

Then I heard more rumors about old friends who had developed new habits. I heard about what was happening to this or that person, and I never had the chance to find out if these things were true. Some of my very best friends growing up were still attending my old school, but I never saw them again. Looking back, I wish I hadn't let rumors prevent me from keeping in touch. I wish I hadn't let what other people thought stop me from investing in important relationships. But that is what fear does to us. It paralyzes us and keeps us from doing the things we know we should.

I wish I could say I've stopped listening to rumors altogether—but that's one of the hardest things in the whole world to do. Rumors still circulate in my world, and sometimes I listen. I tune in to what people are saying about me, even though my experience tells me I shouldn't. When I listen, I find myself hungry to know more, but the hunger is never satisfied. With every morsel of rumor, every taste of "he said" and "she said," every bite of bitterness, I get hungrier. I'm seemingly famished without cure. I ask myself, "Why do I want people from my old high school to see me now? Why do I still wish I could explain why the Alvis sisters disappeared from Newark High School after the summer of 1994?" It's because I'm still letting the rumors affect me.

God wants to fill our whole lives with fruit, but I still allow others to fill my life with doubt. Remember those fruits of the Spirit that God wants to give us? Love. Peace. Joy. Patience. Kindness. Goodness. Faithfulness. Gentleness. Self-control. Nowhere does the Bible say God wants to bring us doubt, fear, envy, or chaos. Listening to rumors and gossip limits our ability to grow and produce good fruit, because the voice of the Holy Spirit gets lost in our low self-esteem and negative worrying.

Have you ever listened to a rumor and let it affect you? Have you ever been hurt by angry words? Have you ever overheard something about you in a conversation that made you doubt and wonder if you really were the person you thought? Dumb questions, I know. Of course you have! We all have.

A better question might be this one: Are you searching for something to give you meaning and purpose after you've tried just about everything and realized nothing works? I know I have. I know the search for meaning and purpose never ends unless we surrender our lives and hearts to the living God who gives us meaning in the body of Christ and who fills our hunger to be significant.

God promises to give us new life and to provide for every need we have: "Ask and it will be given to you; seek and you will find; knock and the door will be opened to you. For everyone who asks receives; those who seek find; and to those who knock, the door will be opened" (Matthew 7:7-8). We can discover a "promised land" of purpose and have lives filled with fruit. All we have to do is ask God to water our souls with grace from the Spirit, love from the body of Christ (the Church), and direction from the Word.

That "rumor" is the polar opposite of the messages we sometimes get from our circles of friends (especially when they are mad at us!). But it's absolutely true.

HURTFUL WORDS

There's a really mean game that girls play sometimes that I call, "Let's Tell Each Other the Truth." I don't know where the game came from or who invented it, but it usually starts when one girl say something like this: "How about you tell me the truth, and I'll tell you the truth, and we'll both promise not to get mad or hurt. Okay?" (You know where this is going, don't you?)

Most of the time, this game is started by a girl who has a burning desire to share a piece of her mind with another girl but doesn't want to come off as being a jerk. The idea makes sense to her. If she gets everyone to agree that they'll all tell "the truth" about each other, then the focus won't be on her or the comment she is dying to make. I know it sounds complicated—but if you've ever been in one of these underhanded girl wars, you know what I'm talking about. If you haven't experienced this kind of direct, raw, and brutal truth, be grateful you've been spared.

One of the biggest flaws in this game is that people always get hurt—no matter how much everyone might promise not to. The second flaw...well, why would any of us want to expose ourselves to the brutality of group judgment? It's sad, but I know why we let ourselves get ambushed from time to time. It's because we are so curious about what other people really think of us.

So one night when I was at camp, the girls I was with started playing this game. All the girls were going around the room saying things to one another. Finally, one girl decided to say something to me. Keep in mind you get mixed feelings in a game like this. You know that you're probably not going to like what you hear, but you feel honored that someone has something to say to you. These types of observations say you are visible in the social realm. Even if the goal of the comment it is to tick you off or annoy you somehow, at least you exist. At the same time, you can also feel this thing get stuck in your throat as you wait for the upcoming "honesty"...I think it's called dread. Whatever it is, it's stuck right there in your esophagus causing you to blink more than normal and shift in your seat.

So I sat there with that feeling for a few moments. And then my truth-teller finally came forth with what she wanted to say: "Brook, I think you are really unapproachable."

Silence.

I immediately began thinking about how weird it was for her to say that, since I knew and talked with just about everyone at the camp. But I wanted to hear more. (Curiosity again set me up for the attack.) So I asked, "Why do you think that?"

"Well, it's just, you have this air about you that comes off as you thinking you are better than everyone else." I said, "Okay," and shut up for the rest of the night. And I've never forgotten those words and how much they hurt me. I found myself being extra nice to people that summer in fear that they might judge me "unapproachable." Isn't it crazy how much one person's words can mean to us? Isn't it weird how we take whatever someone says about us as truth, whether it is or not?

I couldn't see that the person who said those words was probably hurting and confused, that her words came from a desire to be loved and accepted, and that she might have wanted to find some way to make me feel less confident. I don't think she wanted to hurt me, I think she wanted me to believe something about myself that wasn't true because she knew it would affect my actions and my confidence. But all I could hear were her hurtful words.

Let's flip the idea of this around a bit. What if we listened to what God said about us as closely as we listen to the words of our friends (and so-called friends)? It's a huge question.

When I ask myself this question, I have to acknowledge that it's something I still struggle with. I do listen to what other people say about me more intently. Too often, I don't take seriously the words God says about me—you know, the ones that say that I'm beloved, that I have a calling, that I'm pure, that I'm worthy and valuable. Too often I don't really hear it when God says that I matter and my dreams matter, that my life counts in the world, and that my compassion will stem from Christ's. Sometimes it's hard for me to hear the words that tell me not to give up because we have a power within us that is far greater than the powers and principalities of this world.

God wants to fill our lives with fruit, but we've got to listen to the right whispers. There will be times when someone might say something critical that has a bit of truth to it. Constructive criticism from a parent or trusted friend can help us grow. There are always moments when we should pay attention.

But there are many more times that we should turn our ears away from the rumors to hear what the voice of the Spirit tells us. When we attune our ears to God's voice, when we really listen to what God tells us, we begin to see ourselves as we really are.

Set your heart to believing these promises from God about who you really are:

You are a new creation (2 Corinthians 5:17-21).

You are a child of God (John 1:12-13).

God is your friend (John 15:15).

God loves you (John 15:9).

God promises you joy (John 15:11).

You will share in God's glory (John 17:22).

You will share in Jesus' risen life (Colossians 3:1-4).

You will share in Jesus' inheritance (Romans 8:17).

You will share in his future reign...this means you are royalty (Revelation 3:21).

You can dwell in God's presence knowing you are protected and safe (Psalm 91).

You are fearfully and wonderfully made (Psalm 139:14).

With the knowledge that you are deeply loved by God, you can begin to dream the dreams that fall in line with the passions and gifts God has given you. So listen to the whispers of God. You'll find that God's words aren't just rumors. They are truth that will give meaning to your dreams and peace to your heart.

YOUR CONFESSIONS

Have you ever been the subject of a rumor? How did it make you feel? Did it cause you to act differently or think differently about yourself?

Read and reflect on the following passage of Scripture:

Good friend, take to heart what I'm telling you; collect my counsels and guard them with your life. Tune your ears to the world of Wisdom; set your heart on a life of Understanding. That's right—if you make Insight your priority, searching for it like a prospector panning for gold, believe me, before you know it Fear-of-God will be yours; and you'll have come upon the Knowledge of God.

(Proverbs 2:1-7, *The Message, Remix*)

What does the knowledge spoken about in this passage mean to you? How does this knowledge affect your life right now?

God tells us wisdom is available to us all. Where do we receive this wisdom?

Send a message to yourself online reminding yourself of one of God's promises. Reply or comment in response to it if you can.

REPLACEMENT

CONFESSION: WHEN IT COMES TO REPLACING THINGS, I'VE GOT IT ALL WRONG. I REPLACE CLOTHING, SHOES, SONGS ON MY iPOD, AND MySPACE LAYOUTS SO QUICKLY THAT YOU'D THINK MY LIFE DEPENDED ON THEM. BUT AS FOR THINGS THAT ARE SUPPOSED TO BE REPLACED REGULARLY (TOOTHBRUSHES, DISPOSABLE RAZORS, MASCARA, ETC.), I ALWAYS WAIT UNTIL THEY ARE ALL FALLING APART AND CRUSTY BEFORE I THROW THEM OUT.

Ice cream is one great way to cope with the side effects of rumors. But I'm pretty sure dealing with the consequences of the negative rumors we sometimes hear will require a bit more from us than just deciding between mint chocolate chip and Rocky Road. These rumors tend to create a hunger that's different from your typical after-school empty stomach. It's a hunger to feel loved, accepted, valuable, and wanted.

I used to try to fill this emptiness with stuff that wasn't necessarily bad, but it definitely wasn't hitting the spot. I would make plans, hang out with people, talk on the phone, read, listen to music, or do homework. These things would fill my day, but they never filled my heart.

How do we cope with the skewed portrayals of ourselves that come from society and what others say about us? One flip through a magazine can send us into a whirlwind of self-doubt, jealousy, and wishful thinking—especially when we don't feel like we fit in. If we are ever to truly live our dreams and become confident in the person God has created, we should start the process of replacing the unhealthy with the healthy, exchanging the bad for the good, trading in an empty heart for a full one.

In middle school the word *replacement* might be used to describe what happens when friends change (like every two days…or every two seconds!) In high school, replacement might mean choosing to hang out with a guy instead of with your girlfriends at the mall. As we move into college, replacement might mean putting away the varsity letter jacket and trying on a college sweatshirt. Beyond college, replacement may mean moving out of your parents' house and starting your own family. We are constantly replacing things throughout our lives. Sometimes replacement feels great; other times, it makes us feel horrible and alone. But this kind of replacement will never give us the satisfaction we truly need.

I was walking through the halls of a local high school a few months ago and was reminded of a really troubling phenomenon. There are people (and we've all been "people" before) who hang around with others in the hallway until their "choice" friends come into sight. I refer to these people as "hallway users." They temporarily use whoever they can to appear not to be alone until the people they really want to hang out with are available. This type of replacement makes us all mad, doesn't it? No one wants to be used or to be the user. But the need for acceptance, the need to fit in, can sometimes outweigh our desire to treat others how we want to be treated.

What's the alternative? What kind of replacement should we seek to avoid hurting others and to be personally satisfied and filled with good things? We need to learn a new method of replacement that will give us a more authentic and lasting confidence—one that will help us remember how valuable we are and will show others how valuable they are. We need to replace the negative "you don't measure up" judgments the world may offer us with the positive "you are valuable and have a purpose" hopes God offers when we open our hearts to them.

Replacing what the world says is true about you (what other people say, what magazines say, what MTV says, etc.) with what God says is true about you (what the Bible says, what the body of Christ says, what the Holy Spirit says to your heart) leads to fulfillment. It quenches this great hunger for acceptance and meaning and gives us a new identity.

Speaking of his connection with God, the psalmist says, "You have been my hope...my confidence since my youth" (Psalm 71:5). God is always available, eager to replace our doubts and fears with great confidence and fruit.

So what does it mean to replace what the world says about us with what God says?

THE WORLD SAYS...	JESUS SAYS...
you must chase after beauty, wealth, and power to be satisfied.	"You're blessed when you've worked up a good appetite for God. He's food and drink in the best meal you'll ever eat" (Matthew 5:6, *The Message Remix*).
no one cares.	I care. Jesus grieves for us (John 11:35).
you are too young to influence anyone.	you have the potential to cleanse, protect, and preserve God's presence in this world—you are salt! (Matthew 5:13).
you are invisible.	you are a light that cannot be hidden, meant to shine before others, "that they may see your good deeds and glorify your Father in heaven" (Matthew 5:14-16).
you have to look and be like everyone else to be loved and accepted.	you can praise God for your uniqueness because you have been fearfully and wonderfully made, by a God who knows and loves you (Psalm 139:14).
you are replaceable.	you are part of the Body, a part that won't go unnoticed. Every gift you have is a part of the whole, the whole that makes up God's kingdom (1 Corinthians 12:12-30).

THE WORLD SAYS...	JESUS SAYS...
you are alone in the world, fending for yourself.	you will never be alone. Jesus sends the Holy Spirit, an advocate and friend to walk with you, guide you, and help keep you from falling away (John 15:26-16:1).
you will be judged for what you are.	Jesus sees you not as you are, but as you can become if you are willing to allow your relationship with him to manage your life (See John 1:42).

REPLACING YOUR CROWN

When I was a festival queen, each weekend I would watch a different queen end her reign by passing her crown on to the new queen who would represent that festival for the next year. At every festival I watched an old queen be replaced with a new one. It's always a weird mixture of feelings to see this happen—and when it was time to give my own crown away, I understood that mix even better. As she passes her crown on, a queen experiences relief that she is finished with her work, and she feels sad it's over. She feels love and gratitude for the friends she's made along the way, yet some jealousy toward the new queen. Finally, she feels like she's being replaced (which she is)—and that can be hard to deal with. That feeling of being replaced can tear you up inside and leave you feeling unnecessary.

But I didn't feel at all unnecessary after I crowned the new queen. Instead, it was a rare moment in which I felt fulfilled. Obviously, I was being replaced—but that didn't make me feel like I no longer mattered. Someone else was going to be carrying on the tradition of amazing Parade of the Hills queens, and she would add her own flavor and gifts to the royal family. I wasn't without value just because I was no longer a festival queen. With all of the new experiences and stories that came from my year as queen, I'd gained a great deal. Those experiences added something new to what I had to offer, and I'm always thankful for that.

When you allow God's voice to replace the whispers of the world, the same thing happens. You become more valuable. You have a new story to tell. Some old patterns in your life are replaced by new ones, but the person you are and the person you've always been is not only alive and well but filled with new reasons to be confident and new reasons to keep telling your stories and living your dreams.

I passed my crown on to a girl named Ashley—and I no longer wear a ten-pound ring of cubic zirconium around on my head. But I know I have a great inheritance in heaven and that God is working in and through me everyday—whether you can see the crown or not. I know in my soul that I am valuable—even though I never participated in another pageant and I never pursued a modeling career beyond that point. I've come to understand a beauty that only God can give, and I'm so glad I didn't listen to the voices that said, "You'll only be beautiful if you win more, get photographed more, or get more friends." I know there is a beauty that exists in me regardless of what other people think. Our dreams are extensions of that beauty that God has created.

Are you waiting for a crown or a place of honor to tell you how much you are loved and accepted? If you are, stop waiting! A place of honor exists for you now, and the assurance of your abundant life in Christ is just a prayer away. God wants you to know how incredibly valuable you are. You've been created to offer the world something only you can give. If you wait for a green light from *CosmoGIRL,* you may spend the rest of your life sitting frozen in the intersection of life staring at a red light. God has created you beautiful, and the dreams God has given you are an extension of that beauty. Go for your dreams.

Allow God to replace the old with the new in your life. He will keep your heart in perfect peace, as long as you trust in him.

YOUR CONFESSIONS

What material possessions have you replaced most recently?

If you could replace one negative thought about yourself, what would it be?

What thoughts do you have about yourself that need to be replaced right now? Complete this sentence for each of those thoughts:

The world tells me _____, but Jesus tells me _____.

What voices do you listen to the most and what are they saying? Do you need to replace the voices you listen to?

REPLACEMENT

Have you ever asked God to replace doubt and fear with new confidence and fruit?

Use the space below to write about your feelings and your desire for a new God-inspired self-understanding.

RISK

Confession: Here's where I bare my soul. (Okay, not really, but here's where I share something really embarrassing, and hope you'll still think I'm respectable, elegant, and not completely ridiculous.) Youth pastors have a tendency to pee their pants. Well, it's not a proven fact... Okay, let's just say I have a tendency to pee my pants. It's the curse of the girl who drinks too much before she goes to bed. This tends to happen at church camp and other really inconvenient places—like when I'm on vacation with my boyfriend. One time during my senior year I was camping in Florida with Coy's family. On the first night I shared a bed with his

TWO YOUNGER SIBLINGS. IN THE MIDDLE OF THE NIGHT, I AWAKENED WITH THE OVERWHELMING URGE TO PEE. IT WAS DARK... I HAD TO CRAWL OVER PEOPLE TO GET OUT OF THE CAMPER... I COULDN'T FIND MY SHOES. THEN I HAD TO WALK A QUARTER MILE TO THE RESTROOMS, AND I TOTALLY PEED MY PANTS BEFORE I GOT THERE. I SPENT AN HOUR WASHING OUT MY CLOTHES AND DRYING THEM WITH THE HAND DRYER, AND THEN CRAWLED BACK INTO BED, ASHAMED AND WORRIED THAT THE FAMILY WOULD ASK WHY I WAS MISSING FOR AN HOUR IN THE MIDDLE OF THE NIGHT.

I KNOW SOMEDAY I'LL PROBABLY HAVE ANOTHER "ACCIDENT" THAT WILL BE IMPOSSIBLE TO CONCEAL...BUT BEING ME, THAT'S JUST THE RISK I LIVE WITH.

Martin Luther King Jr. once said, "Faith is taking the first step, even when you don't see the whole staircase." As we move forward in the journey of life, one step at a time, our individual paths will be illuminated. Our growth in God and our efforts to chase our dreams can be risky, but we don't have to see the whole picture to get going.

One of my high school English teachers used to sing us a song with a similar theme when we were feeling overwhelmed:

Little by little,
Inch by inch,
By the yard, it's hard,
But by the inch, what a cinch!
Never stare up the stairs.
Just step up the steps.

CONFESSIONS OF A Not-So-SUPERMODEL

Little by little,
and inch by inch.

Facing a big project or a major life change requires that we not only stay committed and on course, but also that we risk something. Every time we say yes to a challenge, set a new goal, or try a new way of living, we take a risk. We risk our pride if we fail. We risk our confidence if others see where we came up short. We risk feeling disappointed and incompetent. Life is risky. Yet God calls us to dive into the deep end—floaties and all.

Writing this book is risky business for me. Being a festival queen isn't something most people would put on their resumes or the bios for their ten-year high school reunion. It's awesome when you are in that world, traveling to other festivals and being looked upon by parade lovers. But I have to admit it's kind of quirky and weird to look back on it now and talk about it publicly.

As we move through different stages of our lives, something that might have seemed great one year might suddenly lose its appeal for us. In middle school you might have been very proud of your glittery "I ♥ _____" (fill in the blank) hall pass/student planner. But that isn't something you'd proudly take into homeroom on your first day as a high school freshman. During your senior year you may wear a beautiful and expensive class ring that signifies your various extracurricular activities, but you probably wouldn't wear it to orientation at your future college or university.

Talking about my festival queen days reminds me of these things. That special year taught me so much about faith, my friends, and the risks a person has to take to make a difference. But at the time, entering the festival queen competition felt like a huge social risk for me. I'd already done the unimaginable and transferred to a new school my senior year, joined a volleyball team where obvious roles and positions were already claimed, decided to date a boy from a rival school, and started working two jobs at the mall. Entering a beauty competition could have been the icing on the proverbial cake when it came to my declining social status, but I decided to enter anyway. I knew it would make my family proud and give me a goal to work toward.

In my mind, the real risk wasn't that I might not win—I was prepared for that. The real risk was that I might win. Don't misunderstand—I wasn't overly confident or proud. It's just that there were fewer than 20 girls competing that year, and my 5'11" status made it hard to go incognito. I knew there was a possibility I might win, and I didn't want to spend every weekend traveling the Ohio Festival circuit rather than hanging out with friends, sleeping, and doing homework. I honestly didn't know how I would cope if I won the competition. But having taken the risk all by myself, I had to accept the outcome.

After I won, the reality of my next year sunk in like one of those sink holes that happen underneath homes in Central Florida. The sand below the foundation collapses, creating a hole the size of a small car. Often, this hole comes unannounced and leaves a family feeling confused and afraid (and sometimes even without a home). This was my state of mind when I won the title of Miss Parade of the Hills. With the crown came new responsibilities and accountability. I had to travel and represent our festival. I risked being ridiculed at school for missing practices and social events because of festival functions. I found myself wondering if I could finish out the year—and why I'd ever entered the contest in the first place.

I'm able to see now how God used the risk I took in entering that funny little festival to make me a better person, a better lover of people, and a more grateful citizen. Looking back, the risk was worth it. It changed me and increased the measure of my faith.

The life of faith can be a risk. Our desire to follow Christ on this journey can look really odd to those outside of Christianity. Why would we trust in something we may never be able to prove scientifically or understand completely? Why would we seek to fill our hunger with something the world can't see? What do we risk when we make decisions that friends who may be far from God won't understand? Right now, the risks may not seem worth it. Having your social life on the line or having rumors circulating about you may not be your cup of cappuccino—but look at the alternative. What if we never take these risks? What if we don't allow God to guide us through the unexpected turns of life? We are left not only with rumors, but also with dissatisfaction and an emptiness that still needs to be filled.

If I had never become a festival queen I wouldn't have these stories to tell now. I wouldn't be able to share with you how the random moments in our lives can teach us something. What if refusing to take a risk leaves you just as empty as you started?

RISKY BUSINESS

Not listening to rumors, replacing the world's perspective with God's—such behavior is risky, because it requires that we change.

Mother Teresa once said, "From the moment a soul has the grace to know God, she must seek." Consider all the risks Mother Teresa took to know God. She spent her life living among the poorest of the poor, sharing God's love with them. But those risks ultimately led to the greatest fruit of her life. She became a role model, a "supermodel" of grace and a transformed life.

If Mother Teresa tells us we need to seek, then we must! As I've shared earlier, my own seeking didn't lead me down the traditional modeling path I'd imagined since my childhood. But I took a risk to become a supermodel of a different type. It was a risk that required hard work, sacrifice, and the faithful support of my family (and my husband's family). But instead of spending my days at photo shoots, I spent my days in school preparing for ministry. I spent my days in the church hanging out with teenagers, doing my best to model Christ's love for them. Sometimes I've messed up and totally missed the point, but becoming a supermodel continues to be a risk I'm willing to take. I want to be a supermodel of grace, someone who displays the beauty that comes from a life filled with God's grace. My new kind of supermodel lifestyle is a life of purpose, rooted in God's kingdom principles (rather than a life that seeks outward perfection and selfish goals). It might cost me a lot that the world values, but that's a sacrifice I'm willing to make, because God defines who I am, and the fruit of ministry is worthwhile.

What would you be willing to risk your life for? For me, it's teenagers and other people who may need a friend to help them through the rough patches of life. Seeking God is risky, but it's worth every moment. Seeking God leads to dreams that come true.

YOUR CONFESSIONS

What's the biggest risk you've ever taken? Were you nervous? Excited? Scared? How did you deal with these emotions?

What kind of risks do you think people take when they decide to live a Christian lifestyle?

Has it ever been risky for you to seek after God?

How have you sought after God this week? This month? This year?

Have you ever felt afraid to follow God's leading in your life?

If Jesus could go with you anywhere and help you do anything, where would you go and what would you do?

Do you believe Jesus goes with you even now? What holds you back from trusting him?

ROYALTY

CONFESSION: I STILL LOVE DISNEY THEME PARKS. I LIKE GOING INTO THE STORES WHERE YOU CAN BUY PRINCESS DRESSES, SHOES, AND TIARAS. THEY DON'T FIT ME ANYMORE—BUT SOMETIMES I WISH THEY DID.

"But to all who believed him and accepted him, he gave the right to become children of God. They are reborn—not with a physical birth resulting from human passion or plan, but a birth that comes from God."

John 1:12-13 (NLT)

WICKER OR VELVET?

Imagine yourself seated on a throne, the same throne that many queens have sat on before you. What does your throne look like? Mine was a wicker fan chair, one you might see in a 1990s *Baywatch* reunion party or something. They (and by "they" I mean the people in charge of the annual Parade of the Hills festival queen competition) have used the same wicker chair for years, and it really is an honor to be seated there, whether wicker is your thing or not. You may have imagined a more opulent throne, perhaps with velvet, silver, and gold, maybe even an insignia with your initials on the top. That's how I always imagine royalty—seated in overpriced chairs, wearing layers of beautiful fabrics, regularly being given the very best tastes and treasures the world has to offer.

There are still a few places in our world, like England, where royal families are still given such high and exalted treatment. (Whenever I see a picture of Princess Diana on her wedding day, I think of the nightmares those florists and seamstresses must have had!) But in our everyday worlds we don't see too many people afforded this type of majestic existence. So maybe my odd festival queen days are a little closer to how most of us feel—like a teenager on a wicker throne feeling just a bit out of place, riding on a minivan instead of a Mustang, wondering if her bra strap is showing under her formal dress, and hoping she won't fall off a car in the middle of a parade route. There were times when I wondered if a kindergartner could do a better job as festival queen than I was doing.

We've all had dreams about being royalty, about being someone special and beloved. But the truth is, most of us feel out of place most of the time—and never really find this way of life in our real worlds.

Here's the good news. Every single one of us is royalty. Each of us has been promised a throne. You may never have entered a beauty pageant, you may not be scheduled to marry a prince and become queen, but you have a throne that is ready and waiting for you to claim.

But just like my wicker chair wasn't the throne I'd imagined, the throne Christ has promised us if we've given him the opportunity to guide and direct our lives isn't quite like the ones we see in movies. As beloved daughters of God, we have been promised a place of royalty. We've got a spot right next to Jesus. But that spot is not set apart from the world, but immersed in it—right next to Jesus, wherever Jesus may be, partaking in God's promises but also being about God's business.

The big sparkly crown placed on my head when I became festival queen carried with it some pretty big responsibilities. It meant I had to be about the business of the Parade of the Hills every weekend, doing things that reflected all the good and wonderful things that Nelsonville had to offer. It's the same when we are given this divine inheritance, this mission, this awesome blessing of becoming God's beloved children. We are royalty beyond measure, with access to the blessings and promises of a loving and nurturing God. But we also have the responsibility to be about our Father's business, just as Jesus was (See Luke 2:49). Translation: Our throne as daughters of God isn't a chair; it's a way of life. It's a knowledge that compels us to live and to love differently.

So wicker and velvet really don't apply here. We find ourselves asking different questions, like "Is my throne made of kindness and patience, love and self-control?" Are any of these traits sounding familiar? Our lives are a gift from God—and the fruit, the gifts, the blessings, the character God gives us is what we offer to God and the world as we go on representing Jesus.

It's as if Jesus holds a festival and has crowned you the queen. (For the full festival queen experience, imagine that you've also been handed some silk flowers that look like they have water on them but it's really just dried glue, a personalized plaque, an official certificate, and a sash with your name on the back.) Now that you've been adopted queen, you have your whole reign (your whole life!) ahead to travel all over the world sharing about the festival you represent. My reign as Miss Parade of the Hills ended in August of 1997, but my reign as God's child, and God's ambassador of love in the world will never end, as long as I am loyal to the One who gave me all of these gifts.

So the question lingers, what kind of queen have you been lately? I have to admit there were times when I was terrible at being Miss Parade of the Hills. I would roll out of the car in a dazed-and-confused post-nap state and mumble my little speech, and afterward I wasn't even sure if I'd remembered to talk about the fiddlers' competition and the 5K or if I'd accidentally substituted a dirt-bike parade and a Moon-Pie eating contest! On those days, I would feel bad for not having my act together. But there were other days when I nailed that speech on the platform, not just by remembering to mention all the things our festival had to offer, but also by having a genuine passion for something I cared about...our festival.

It's the same with us. You are royalty, and Christ has crowned you a queen. But you'll still have days when you can't even remember the combination to your gym locker, let alone have patience and self-control with a friend who shows up wearing your jeans to school. God asks us to walk as Jesus did. It is our calling, our duty as young women who share an inheritance with Christ. When we believe in Christ, God makes us into our true selves—our "child-of-God" selves. Isn't that an awesome thing to know? We aren't entirely who we think we are. Each of us has the ability to reflect our Creator, the amazing and compassionate God who made the universe.

Knowing this changes everything. It makes us so valuable to the world. It should give you hope...

> *This resurrection life you received from God is not a timid, grave-tending life. It's adventurously expectant, greeting God with a childlike "What's next, Papa?" God's Spirit touches our spirits and confirms who we really are. We know who he is, and we know who we are: Father and children. And we know we are going to get what's coming to us—an unbelievable inheritance! We go through exactly what Christ goes through. If we go through the hard times with him, then we're certainly going to go through the good times with him!*

Romans 8:15-17, *The Message Remix*

A QUEEN'S RIGHTS

There's one common misunderstanding we need to avoid when we use this queenly or royal imagery. It concerns our understanding of what a queen deserves or has rights to.

For example, you may think a queen would have subjects following her around straightening her hair, offering her low-fat organic snacks, making friendship bracelets, and uploading her favorite songs onto her iPod. Maybe you even have some friends who are willing to do all these things for you—perhaps out of love, perhaps out of a desire to be loved and accepted. But I know for sure this isn't the type of relationship Jesus wants us to have with others after we've realized our royal status.

Jesus is our best example of a royal life lived out with a servant's heart. Instead of having his closest followers ceremonially wash his feet, Jesus washes theirs (John 13:3-17). He shows us how to love by taking the form of a servant. And he commands us to live out our royal callings by serving one another in that same way. I am always amazed at this story and the example Jesus set for us to follow.

I've mentioned Mother Teresa earlier, because I think she's a fantastic model for what it means to live out love as Jesus did. Time after time she gave up her own bed, her food, and her security to show love to others—especially those who were most poor and destitute. Imagine if the President of the United States gave up his seat on Air Force One so you could fly out and visit your grandma for Thanksgiving. We don't expect someone with that much money, security, and power to give up that position for someone who has none of these things. Yet this is what Jesus has done for us. Jesus has given us everything we need, and even what we didn't deserve, to express God's great love for us. This knowledge alone brings about a desire to serve God with our whole hearts, minds, and with all of our strength.

In our service to the King, as royal heirs to the throne, we must remember that sometimes the place of honor is the place where we serve others in genuine love and sacrifice.

Have you ever given up something for someone else? Have you ever served a friend or family member when it really cost you something? Maybe it cost you your time, your money, or even your reputation.

We all have something to give. We are all God's beautiful children who reign as royal servants, servants of love.

FUELED BY FAITH

As you think about what it means to live out your dreams in faith, remembers these principles:

1. Following your dreams takes great faith and fullness that is available only through a relationship with God. Asking God to be with you on your journey is the first step in making your dreams become reality.

2. There will always be many voices willing to speak to you about your worth. Listening to God's promises rather than the world's rumors will give you confidence to live a fruitful life.

3. Growing in faith requires replacement. Bad habits, marred self-image, selfish behaviors, or even just listening to the wrong crowd—all these things can be replaced with promises from God that will never fail. Your actions will begin to reflect fruit instead of great hunger.

4. Dreaming for God means taking a risk. Be ready to trust Jesus with the steering wheel of your life, and be willing to follow along wherever he leads.

5. Know who you are. You come from a royal line of believers who know their purpose. Love God with your whole heart and with your actions as well. The fruit that comes to live in your heart will change your life and help enliven your dreams in new ways. Always remember what it says in Psalm 45:11: "The king is enthralled by your beauty; honor him, for he is your Lord."

YOUR CONFESSIONS

You are adopted as God's child, a recipient of a great inheritance of grace. What do you think your response to grace should be?

When and where are you most likely to forget your status as beloved royalty? At school? With friends? During hard times? Explain why it's hard for you to remember who you are in Christ.

Name some ways you could help yourself (and possibly your friends) remember your lineage as daughters of God.

When do you find yourself drifting away from your responsibilities to the throne (or your relationship to Jesus)?

If you could choose your throne of love, the throne where you serve Jesus with your life, what would it look like and where would it be?

FRIENDS

CONFESSION: I MISS THE DAYS OF PASSING NOTES IN
SCHOOL. MY DNEIRF NERAK DNA I DEVOL GNITIRW LLA
FO EHT SDROW SDRAWKCAB. SECRET CODES AND A SHARED
LOVE FOR COLORED PENCILS CAN BE THE SIMPLEST FORM OF
FRIENDSHIP. I STILL HAVE SOME OF THE NOTES KAREN AND
I PASSED IN THE EIGHTH GRADE—THEY MEAN THAT MUCH
TO ME.

I made some fantastic friends while traveling the Ohio festival
circuit. It was a great privilege to get to travel around my home
state learning about the different cultures and traditions in each
town and city. But the added bonus of going to the Jackson
County Apple Festival or the Millersport Sweet Corn Festival
was getting to meet the queens of these festivals. I traveled

with some really amazing girls the year I spent representing the Parade of the Hills, and I learned some really cool lessons along the way.

Friends are important to the development of our faith. Sometimes our dreams can really take off when friends provide encouragement (or even sometimes a good kick in the pants to get us started). I'm writing this book now because my husband and one of my best friends wouldn't let me forget about this dream of writing a book for young women. They wouldn't let me give up. They wouldn't take no for an answer. They refused to accept my rationalizations and all the reasons why I hadn't started working toward my dreams. It can be frustrating and even annoying when a friend tries to help, but it's also one of the most valuable gifts you can ever receive, to be loved in a way that challenges you to press forward in deepening your faith and going after your dreams. Friends can give us a special dose of courage and even help us to see where we are falling short.

Growing up, your best friend is the girl who spends the night at your house, and you spend the night at hers. Best friends talk on the phone for hours. They can finish each other's sentences. A friend who has known you since childhood can remind you of the day when your family pet died and how she made you feel better by making you laugh all night long. These are the types of friendships we cherish and protect. Friends offer us relief, protection, camaraderie, shared aims, support, joy, and encouragement. And sometimes, if you're lucky, your friends will challenge you to grow.

Experiencing friendship has been a medicine for my soul. My best friends know me and accept me no matter how lame I become (or was to begin with)! With these friends there's a level of trust that allows me to share my feelings and fears, without ever wondering if they might judge me or decide not to be my friend because of what I've said. There's a love you can experience in friendship that's really uplifting, and it makes you want to return it—you want to give some back.

Good friends are there when we need a shoulder to cry on or an ear that will listen to us. We need friends to share moments of spontaneous fun and even embarrassment.

One of my very best childhood friends shared my love for music. We used to stay up all night listening to her CD collection. Sometimes we'd make up our own songs. I remember a time when we were in middle school, and I joined her family on vacation (during a particularly hard time in my own family life). We were driving along in the van listening to Rod Stewart's song, "Have I Told You Lately That I Love You," and we both started crying. I don't think either one of us knew why we were crying, but we cried together, and that was all that mattered.

She understood the dynamics in my family, and I understood hers. I loved how we could laugh at the smallest things or pig out on zucchini bread in her kitchen. Her friendship was a haven for me during my adolescence. All of us need these kinds of friendships to give us joy, comfort, and support.

We also need friends to help us on the journey of faith. A friend of mine in high school helped me on my journey. She had a lot of this "fruit stuff" we've been talking about.

Meet Courtney.

Courtney was part of the small youth group my sister and I joined in Newark, Ohio. My family was going through a rough time, and my mom had encouraged us to go to church. Courtney and her friend Ashley were among the first girls we met there. They were outgoing and nice. They introduced themselves to us right away and made us feel comfortable. During that first youth group meeting, Courtney prayed out loud. During her prayer I heard her ask God to bless her friends. Not only was she not ashamed to pray aloud at church, but she also wasn't afraid to talk to God about the things going on in her life. Afterward, she asked my sister and me if we knew about summer camp. Before we left, we had brochures and camp information in our hands. We ended up going to camp that summer, which changed the whole course and direction of my life.

Courtney's enthusiasm was contagious. The fruit in her life led me to trust her and, eventually, to trust in God.

There was a cool chemistry in our friendship. We could talk about serious things—life, faith, family, and friends—but we could also stay up until 3 a.m. joking around, telling stories about our childhoods, and making food. When it came to spiritual matters, she was always there to listen or help if she could. One of the remarkable things about Courtney was that she wasn't afraid to show her weaknesses. Even though she was a lot more mature in her faith than I was, she still had struggles, and she wasn't afraid to talk about them and let me or other friends help her. I learned a lot from this friendship.

Courtney helped me see that we are all part of the body of Christ, the church. God's Spirit lives in each one of us, and we lose a great deal if we overlook it. Friends are important. They can weaken us or strengthen us.

Ecclesiastes tells us that two standing together are stronger than one, and that a cord of three strands is not easily broken (Ecclesiastes 4:9,12). Have you ever tried to pull a rope apart with your bare hands? (I struggle pulling the tags off my new clothes!) There's no way I can break a rope that has been woven together. In that same way, God wants our lives to be intermingled with the lives of other followers. We strengthen one another by sticking together. We are stronger when we choose friends who will keep us accountable, protect us when we are weak, laugh with us when we goof up, and cry with us when we are broken. These types of friends deserve our time, our energy, and our love.

Good friends can help keep each other sharp, just as iron sharpens iron (Proverbs 27:17). A friend can strengthen you and encourage you to keep going after your dreams and your faith. That's why it's so important to be wise about who you choose to be your closest friends.

People often say good friends stick together, and that's true. When you think about it, sticking together can mean all kinds of things. Friends can stick together physically, so no one is tempted to go to the "punch" bowl at the party or go home with that guy in his car. Friends can stick together spiritually by sharing concerns, burdens, and temptations and praying for one another. Friends can stick together emotionally by believing in one another through both the tough times and the times when things are going great.

What if we all embraced this type of living? Instead of judging a friend who struggles or fails, God calls us to help her back on her feet and restore her to faith by encouraging, forgiving, and loving. And within the body of Christ, others will offer us that same loving support. God uses our strengths to build up the body and allows us to be a way for grace to enter into one another's struggles.

COUNTRY PARTY

I remember a time when my friends were having a party down a little country road in Ohio. The party was supposed to last all night. And the plan was for everyone to sleep outside (both guys and girls). The guys were going to sleep in tents, but the girls were all going to sleep on the trampoline (maybe because it was far off the ground, away from bugs and snakes). I remember that the guys took turns grabbing an electric fence that kept the cows in, and we watched their feet light up. (Genius, right?) A few of my girlfriends kept disappearing into the woods. Some of the girls would go alone. Looking back on that night, the girls who stayed together on the trampoline remember an evening of laughter and fun. For some of the other girls, the next morning was blurry with hangovers and partial memories about what they did or didn't do in the woods. I was sad that I didn't try to talk them into staying with us. Maybe it wouldn't have made a difference. But I knew that having friends around me that night kept me safe.

For someone like me, a person who often searched for male approval, it would have been a bad deal for me to be alone with a guy in the woods. I was glad I was with girlfriends who knew my values well. My friends could remind me of these values in a moment of weakness. That night could have been very different without my friends.

God knows that we need help to stay strong in living out our faith. Close friends who will walk beside us are one gift that can strengthen us. Where do you stand with your friends? Are your friends a positive and encouraging support to you or a group where you constantly find yourself being tempted? You don't need to ditch someone as a friend because she doesn't share your values. But you do need to have a different mindset when you are around people who tend to head in a different direction from where we would like to go. Friends who back us, support us, love us, and help us—and even love our friends who aren't the greatest examples—are good ones to surround ourselves with.

How can you get friends like that? The first step is seeking to be that kind of friend to others. The example you set will be contagious and the Spirit will bless your relationships. The identity you find in Christ will help you understand your connections to the Body (other people). So, start by identifying the friends you have who strengthen your relationship with God, your commitment to church or to purity. Hang on to friends who won't judge but will help you remain faithful to your values. And do the same for those friends, by finding out what matters most to them and helping them stay on track.

Knowing someone has your back is such a freeing feeling. And, knowing that you are your sister's keeper is a responsibility that will make you more aware in situations that could lead to compromise.

God gives us grace so we can love the friends God brings into our lives. Out of that love, God sometimes brings forth some of the coolest relationships, the ones we aren't expecting, the ones that last.

I wasn't expecting to meet a lifelong friend at a dinner during a youth workers' convention in Dallas, Texas. I sat next to someone I didn't know, but our interests were similar, and we found common ground right away. All it took was one conversation and a commitment to stay in touch. Today, she is one of those people in my life I wouldn't want to live without. God brings us the people we need—and sometimes leads us to people who need us.

Several years ago, I started working out with one of my small group leaders at the gym. We took a crazy Latin music/Hip Hop aerobics class together. It was psycho and hilarious, but we took it seriously and tried not to miss our workouts together. Out of that experience we developed a friendship for life, one that challenges and blesses me more than I can say. What started with some Beyonce dance moves and a burrito dinner afterward turned into a blessing only God could give—friendship.

Have you found a friendship like this yet? Don't worry if you haven't. God will bring the right people your way. At the same time, always be looking for opportunities to be the friend God is calling you to be. We have a great opportunity to love and to build up the body of Christ through friendship.

SISTER, SISTER

When I was growing up, there was a TV show called *Sister, Sister* that I used to watch every day after school for a while. Tia and Tamara were twin sisters who were always finding themselves in funny or difficult situations. Often, one or both of them would make a bad choice. Their mom would usually find out, and there was always some kind of consequence or lesson to be learned. The specifics of the setting and the choices were always changing, but there was one thing you could count on every episode. No matter how much Tia and Tamara disagreed with each other (and sometimes even disliked each other), they were always there to support and protect each other, even if things had gone badly. They were tight. Nothing could tear them apart. They fought, had moments of doubt, and even wondered whether to stick up for each other at times. But these sisters always came to the same conclusion: We are family, and we are meant to take care of each other.

Like Tia and Tamara, we are meant to live alongside our friends, helping and encouraging each other, even when it's hard. God has given us many sisters. We may not always agree or do the right things, but we are always connected by the love of God. Living out of this love, we learn to care (and care deeply) for one another.

YOUR CONFESSIONS

What does the word accountability *mean to you?*

Do you have a friend you can trust enough to keep you accountable?

When are you weakest spiritually around your friends? When are you strongest spiritually around your friends?

What traits would your ideal best friend have? Do you have those traits?

Ask God to help you make great friends and to teach you how to love.

ADD ME

Confession: I have "issues"—and one of them is a serious and unhealthy addiction to checking e-mail, text messages, online community posts, and voicemail. Could it be that MySpace rehabilitation centers will pop up in the near future?

"I don't want to gain the whole world and lose my soul."
tobyMac, "Lose My Soul," *Portable Sounds* (Forefront Records, 2007)

LOOKING FOR LOVE IN ALL THE WRONG PLACES

The move from elementary school to middle school is a big transition for most of us. For me, graduation from the fifth grade tossed me from the comfort of my small elementary school into a larger middle school full of new faces and experiences. The "popular" girls from our elementary school had to battle for territory with popular groups from the other elementary schools that joined with ours. I wasn't particularly popular, but I knew that the switch to a new school gave us all a new chance—a chance to prove our worthiness to receive masses of school pictures. (You know, the wallet size photos that you hand out to all your friends with little notes on the back like "love ya like a sis" and "to a really cute boy.") I was hoping to get lots of pictures that year from lots of new friends.

But there was one problem. It could be explained in one word (or, more accurately, one brand): K-Swiss. Yes, pass or fail on the "popular list" depended on what kind of footwear you were wearing on the first day of school that year. The summer before I started sixth grade, the importance of having pristine white sneakers with the royal symbol of K-Swiss was impressed on our young minds via magazines, malls, and good marketing. For the first time, I became name-brand conscious, understanding that having the right logo can bring you temporary joy, approval, and satisfaction.

Not much has changed since I was in the sixth grade. Brand-conscious teenagers still spend a lot of money and energy being fashionably in season. It's an expensive trap, one that can hurt the heart and the wallet.

My wallet never had much in it to begin with, and my hard-working parents didn't have the extra money to dish out for the latest K-Swiss. So I settled for a pair of white Reeboks from JCPenney that I would end up wearing most of the year, while everyone else's K-Swiss were getting upgraded to the new editions. By the time some of us finally got our first pair of white K-Swiss sneakers, anyone who was anyone had moved on to brown leather Eastlands. In fact, I could definitely chronicle my whole middle school and high school career with the type of shoe everyone was wearing each semester. K-Swiss, Eastland Oxfords, Timberlands (or Esprit Boots), Air Max, Birkenstocks, Nike Tailwinds...the seasons were and are still never-ending.

I get sad thinking about the things I wanted—things I thought would open up doors of acceptance and reassurance for me. It's puzzling how something like having the right pair of shoes can briefly usher in feelings of worthiness. But in our consumer culture, the problem with shoes is that they quickly go out of style. There is never a moment when you can be on the cutting edge and on top of the fashion world, no matter how hard you try! Celebrities can't even do it, and most of them hire someone to help them try!

So why do we think material things will get us the love and acceptance that we long for? Buying a new iPod or getting that new designer bag may satisfy us and our watching world for a moment, but what happens when the new and improved iPod comes out a few months later? What happens when the bag you bought isn't the latest design? What happens when you get tired of keeping up? We all face these pressures, and they will steal our joy, if we let them.

It's important to recognize that it's natural for us to want love and acceptance. Love and acceptance are good things. However, if the search for love and acceptance becomes our focus, it's easy to end up finding the wrong things to fill us. Jesus urges us to trust him to provide what we need:

> *Therefore I tell you, do not worry about your life, what you will eat or drink; or about your body, what you will wear...look at the birds of the air; they do not sow or reap or store away in barns and yet your heavenly Father feeds them. Are you not much more valuable then they?*
>
> *Matthew 6:25-27*

God wants to free us from our worries and our fears. But the truth is, we have to be willing to seek God first, to seek God's kingdom, to strive to live as Jesus did, and to follow after God's righteousness with all of our hearts. When we do this, God sees our hearts and will provide us with everything we need.

NO, REALLY, ADD ME—PLEASE!

MySpace is a huge online community right now that allows you to connect with people all over the world. One key function of MySpace is adding friends to your page—and requesting that others add you to their pages. We want to be "added" so desperately. It's always kind of a downer when I log on and there aren't any new friend requests in my profile. I have hundreds of friends, students, and family members on the site, and I only have time to talk to a few of them. But their existence as "my friends" comforts me and makes me feel loved. How many friends can I get? How many adds can I get? Will you add me? Will you be my friend? Like the things we buy to gain acceptance, things like MySpace can fill our hearts with overwhelming urges to gain more friends, more comments, more affirmation (genuine or not).

MySpace can tempt us to value quantity over quality in relationships. The focus is on getting more friends, not making the friendships we have better. I love the way MySpace allows me to stay in touch with people, to share updated pictures and stories with a larger group of people than might be possible otherwise. But I must constantly remember to invest in others every day in real life, to love the friends I have and to work on the relationships I have, making them deeper and more authentic.

When I step back and think about those early days in middle school, I realize that my real friends cared nothing about my shoes or my sweet side bangs. The friends I love and cherish today are the ones I stayed up all night with sharing secrets and ordering Chinese food. Friendship is vital to our growth and to our spirituality, but we can pay a high price for artificial friendships. Often the friends we really need are the ones who are already sitting on our bedroom floors with us, trying to figure out the same things we are. How can I get enough money to get my nails done this month? But also, how am I going to get "his" attention this week? Do I matter? Will anyone love me?

As young women, our struggles often revolve around

- friends

- boys

- appearance

- grades

- involvement in sports, dance, or other activities

- family stress

- clothes and accessories

But truly, underneath all these is an inner struggle. The question that begs to be answered is, *Am I good enough?* Have I met the requirements to be part of the group? Our desire to be accepted and admired is so strong that we may be tempted to try whatever seems to be working for everyone else (buying more stuff, updating our look, being at all the right places and with the right people, dating the right guys, going to the best parties). It doesn't matter what group you hang out with—all come with certain requirements (both spoken and unspoken). The choice often comes down to what you value and respect most. Is the desire to be "added" greater than your desire to be who you have been created to be?

There is no easy answer to all of this. However, there is a truth that many people who know Christ have come to rely on. It is this realization: You don't have to be defined by the world. The world will call the shots all day long when it comes to your hair, friends, and decision-making, especially if your goal is to gain its approval. But as your focus shifts from gaining the approval of the world around you to gaining the approval of a loving and forgiving God, your life changes. You are added into a new family of "friends" who will never take you off their "top 8" or change their minds about you. When you place your faith in Jesus, you become one of the family. When you believe in Jesus, you inherit all the riches that come with knowing him (Romans 8:16-17). When you trust in Jesus you find that you feel loved and accepted, even when the people around you aren't so accepting. Knowing Jesus is a powerful thing.

REMEMBERING YOUR TRUE CHILD-OF-GOD SELF

It's so easy to forget your worth when the world is able to get so much of your attention and time. There is no way to remove yourself entirely from the influences that tell you that you have to buy your worth or do something for it. But there are tools we can use every day to remind ourselves of our true nature as beloved children of God...

Confession:

We tend to think of confession in terms of admitting our shortcomings—and this is important. But God wants intimacy with you and wants to give you peace. Telling God your fears and frustrations isn't going to hurt God's feelings. So go for it, let it all out. You can journal (this is my favorite type of prayer). You can even yell your prayers into the sky in your backyard. You can text message God. (Just don't send it to anyone by accident!) Try writing a song or a poem to express your feelings.

Scripture:

Put little reminders of who you are in Christ on your bathroom mirror. Place Bible verses in your car or in your locker. Set yourself up to be reminded regularly of the promises that never fail. So when you are really in those "desert times" you'll have something to remind you of your worth and of the fruit that is available to you if your heart is ready to receive it.

Listening:

Spending time in meditation may not seem like the coolest Friday night activity. But you don't have to bring out the candles and the yoga mat to meditate. You can listen to God in a brief moment. You can listen to God when reading your Bible or a book that is challenging to your faith. Intentionally keeping your mind open to the Holy Spirit can bring you a new sensitivity and a new understanding of your worth. Silence and solitude are artifacts these days. Take a few minutes before dinner, before practice, before bed—whenever you have time—to breathe, to listen, to hear God's voice, to focus on nothing but being available.

Reading:

Read God's Word out loud. Read it silently. Read it over and over again. God can speak to you in new ways through a verse you've heard your whole life. Give God a chance to teach you something. Our minds are saturated with images and messages from every place under the sun. But when we read the Bible and seek to know Jesus more fully, God gives us new understanding of how and why we are here. Don't neglect the Word that gives us life.

But it's not just Scripture that can encourage and challenge us to grow. There are all kinds of books out there that can keep you grounded in your faith, help you through struggles, make you laugh, and give you new perspective. Seek out good books that will help balance your soul. (Check out other Invert Books from Zondervan at your local Christian bookstore or at www.zondervan.com. They are written with you in mind.)

Communion and Fellowship:

God has given us a very special gift—each other! Seriously, I'm so grateful that I had a couple of godly friends in high school. It was their friendship and example that gave me the courage to give God a try. And I continue to rely on other Christians to help me through the tough times and to celebrate with me when things are good. We will always have moments of weakness, struggle, or crisis. I don't think I've ever had a day when every single thing went right. This is why we need each other. We lean on one another during the ups and downs of life. When you are weak, your Christlike friends may be able to help you see realities and truths from God that your situation has prevented you from seeing. Ask your Christian friends for help, and be a friend when someone else is in need.

Service:

Serving others opens our hearts to people and ministers to the body of Christ. When we spend time focusing on the needs of others, we begin to see our own needs and the burdens that go with them in a different light. The hope of others is something contagious that can nourish our own souls.

YOUR CONFESSIONS

Do you find yourself judging your worth based on things like comments on MySpace or Facebook, or even how many text messages you get in a day?

When have you felt the need for something more than external approval from others?

How do you deal with feelings of loneliness?

What is the most insane thing you've done to gain a friend? Was it worth it?

Describe how you feel about yourself apart from your friends.

Do you need God's love and grace to redefine your view of yourself?

LOVE ME

CONFESSION: IT TOOK ME A LONG TIME TO REALIZE THERE WAS A HOLE INSIDE MY HEART THAT ONLY GOD COULD FILL. IN FACT, I STILL STRUGGLE WITH THIS KNOWLEDGE AND TRY TO FIT OTHER THINGS WHERE ONLY GOD AND GOD'S PROMISES FIT PERFECTLY. EVERY DAY IS A NEW OPPORTUNITY FOR ME TO ASK FOR HELP IN GRASPING THIS. EVERY DAY IS A NEW OPPORTUNITY TO YIELD TO THE SPIRIT BY SAYING, "OKAY, YOU'RE IT. YOU'RE THE ONLY THING I NEED."

———

We've all heard of the Ten Commandments. But sometimes I wonder if there should have been one more—at least for me: *Thou shalt not drive while doing the hand motions to popular church songs.* I learned the hard way that songs like "Waves of Mercy," "Father Abraham," "Pharaoh Pharaoh," and "Big House" should be reserved for wide-open spaces.

You see, I was the oldest kid in our family. So of course, I was bestowed with all the finest "oldest child" privileges. One of those privileges, once I was old enough to get my driver's license, was being the driver for our school carpool. Every day I would drive my three younger siblings (two sisters and a brother) and two innocent neighbor kids to and from school. For the most part, I was a pretty responsible driver; however, there were times when I was so glad to be going home that we'd crank up the family-friendly kid music and fly home like Ricky Bobby in *Talladega Nights.*

One day, our little car party didn't turn out so awesome. We were cruising along, singing a verse of "Pharaoh, Pharaoh, Oh, baby, let my people go," when we (I) ran over a set of Ohio-country-road railroad tracks. These weren't your ordinary rattle-the-tires type of tracks. These were the kind where you need to slow down to about 10 mph to avoid bottoming out on the other side. We were going close to 40, maybe 50 mph. (I was really hyper and excited to be going home—which doesn't make it okay.)

So we hit the tracks like a ski jump and took flight into mid-air. All I could do was hold the wheel tightly, hoping we wouldn't crash into the deep ditches located on both sides of the narrow road. We hit the ground with a thud and some crunchy scraping noises. Something under our car made contact with the road below (could it have been the engine?) causing us all to bounce into the air again and back down a second time.

Miraculously, by the grace of our protecting God, the car stayed straight. The car lurched forward painfully, but everything was intact—and we were alive! My nine-year-old sister in the back seat was whimpering with tears of fear. (I think she'd hit her head on the ceiling.) My other sister in the front seat looked at me in shock. The other two kids were speechless. I'm sure they had no faith in me at that point. I laughed an uneasy sigh of relief, and Betsy (the sis in the front) joined in hesitatingly.

Today, we laugh about this little incident—and I thank God I never killed anyone on those travels home from school in the wind and ice and rain. (There was only one other scary moment when, after youth group, I was driving our family minivan on an icy road and managed to do a little 360. But that was it...I think.) I started being more careful.

I used to love listening to music and losing myself in "la la land" during our car rides home. Somehow, the music in the car could transform my state of mind, my mood, and my outlook. Unfortunately, sometimes I seemed to forget that I had a huge responsibility to love and protect those others who were riding with me. Loving the people in my car was more important than paying attention only to my own needs. When we focus so much on our own needs and desires that we forget about the needs of others, we become empty again—selfish and barren of fruit.

When our lives cry out, "Love me, please!" we may be forgetting that God has called us to love one another first.

WHERE DOES LOVE COME FROM?

You may be wondering how it's possible to love others more if we feel like we don't have any love to give, if we are empty to begin with. This is a valid point. It's hard to give out of nothingness. Which leads us to returning to the source of fruit, the true vine of which we are all branches—Jesus.

Every gardener knows that growing fruit can be difficult. It takes time and nurture from God. In the same way, it's not easy to move from a "love me" attitude to an "I love you" attitude. But it begins with learning to trust that it is God's love, first and foremost, that gives us meaning.

The path of loving others isn't easy. Jesus proved that himself when he was in ministry here on earth. It was his love for others that led him to the cross. He knew how hard it was to walk the path of love. Aren't you glad we don't serve a God who has no idea what it means to struggle?

Jesus calls each of us to carry our own cross, much like he did, but he promised never to leave us alone to struggle by ourselves. Each of us has a different cross to carry, one that is uniquely suited to our personality, our gifts, and our callings. Right now, my cross is to be a good wife and mom, a youth pastor students can trust, a good friend, and faithful daughter. Writing this book is also part of what God has asked of me. Each one of us has a role in God's kingdom, filled with opportunities where God can fill our hearts with love—if we could just see that it's not all about us.

Every day presents a new challenge to achieve the love and acceptance of others. Whether it's the affirmation of teachers for our good grades, the attention of boyfriends who notice what we wear each day, or the security that comes from making a team or squad, the quest for acceptance is always before us. We are all looking for that something to make us feel loved. But when our plans to fill the acceptance hole in our hearts go crooked, we sense the emptiness that was there all along.

I can think of all kinds of examples ranging from simple everyday surprises to lifelong disappointments. Imagine you've got a new shirt that you love. You can't wait to wear it to school. But then someone else shows up that day with new jeans or a new bag that completely overshadows your new shirt and your glowing mood. She's basking in what I like to call the "love-light,"—and even though the attention may only last for a day (or just a couple of minutes), it's long enough to make you feel second rate. Maybe it makes you throw up your hands and ask, "Why even try?" Or maybe it just challenges you to try even harder to be noticed and accepted.

So often our efforts scream out to the world, "Love me! Love me!" And when our efforts with clothes and our outward appearance aren't working, we may move on to other things...

THE HAZARDS OF HOUSE-SITTING

I remember when I first realized my search for love and acceptance could lead to compromising situations. I was in the eighth grade and a friend invited me to housesit with her. When we got to the house, she told me she'd invited her boyfriend over. I didn't realize it at the time, but she'd told him to bring a friend so I wouldn't feel alone when she and her boyfriend disappeared. After the guys got there, we watched a movie, and I sat awkwardly next to this guy who barely knew me. Eventually, my friend exited into a nearby bedroom with her boyfriend, leaving me with "random boy"—who was becoming increasingly interested in kissing me. It was only midnight, and our parents weren't expecting us to come home. So there I sat, freaking out inside and wondering how I was going to keep this guy off me for the next eight hours. I ended up pretending to sleep most of the night to get out of this awkward situation. I didn't want to call home and get my friend in trouble, but I really wanted to leave. And, in fact, I should have done just that.

Sometimes our need for acceptance from others pulls so strongly at our hearts that our decision-making becomes less wise and more based on our emotions than anything else. Thankfully, the outcome of that house-sitting night wasn't too bad. I made a good choice, but I struggled all night long, fearing I would be judged for it. But as I went through high school, I was continually faced with the choice: Would I follow the lead of my experienced friends and begin trying "new and exciting" things that were outside of my moral and spiritual boundaries? Or would I risk being different?

Each of us must look in the mirror and acknowledge, "If I stay strong in my faith, I may risk being different." As Christians, when we choose to do our best at living like our true selves, our child-of-God selves, we will be different. This can be hard to accept unless your hearts are filled with the fruit of the Spirit. We can easily get lost in the fog of doubt. Being different without the knowledge of God's love, protection, and peace can leave us feeling alone and vulnerable. And in that state, if we don't find that affirmation and fulfillment in the right places, we can end up compromising.

One night at a recent youth group meeting, I was talking with a group of girls about what kinds of things can cause us to compromise our values. It was an evening when only girls showed up—Lauren, Mekenzie, Becca, Jackie, Katie, and Victoria—so I decided to ditch my lesson and spend time talking about whatever the girls wanted to talk about. We ended up talking about what makes them feel *most beautiful.* The shared answer among the girls that night was *"guys."* I wasn't shocked by this, but I was caught off guard when the girls quickly added that guys also make them feel *most ugly.*

I immediately agreed—and it suddenly made sense to me why many girls feel so empty. A lot of us draw our feelings of beauty and worth from guys—a group of people we can't control and can't always trust to be 100 percent honest with us. After all, guys are human, too, they've got their own struggles and issues, and they have their reasons for acting the way they do (even when they don't know what those reasons are!). We girls end up seeking our feelings of love, beauty, and worth from human beings who, most of the time, don't even realize we're seeking this from them! No wonder we have trouble feeling loved and beautiful!

WHAT IS "IT"?

So what is it that gets in the way of you feeling loved? Seriously, what is "it" for you? If your "it" isn't guys, then it's probably something else.

I've seen so many young women go through a change in late middle school or early high school. They go from knowing they are loved and accepted by God to not being sure of anything at all and wondering where God is in all the darkness. So many young people come to our group in middle school with a crystal-clear understanding of a God who loves them so much. I watch them come to youth group and worship with a passion that is fueled by the knowledge of a Christ who gave up everything for them and a Spirit they trust with their hopes and fears and dreams and discoveries. It's awesome to watch teenagers worship—and I don't just mean singing either, even though the students in my youth group are amazing worshipers in this way. (One guy in my group, Billy Ray, really knows how to sing his praises to God. I've known him to take off his shoes, turn off his cell phone, and seek God with everything he has when the band starts playing.) But these kids worship with their entire lives. They worship through the way they support their friends with prayer and love. They worship through the things they choose to do in their spare time from mission trips to cleaning up parks. I love seeing their faith in action.

But there's often this very visible time occurring sometime in late middle school or in early high school when most girls (and guys, too) seem to find their faith doesn't make much sense anymore. They increasingly see themselves as making their own decisions apart from their parents and begin to wonder if the life of faith is really for them.

One of the best young leaders in my youth group went through such a time recently. She's always had a strong faith. She's attended Christian summer camp for as long as she can remember and has been on every church mission trip since she joined the youth group. She does her best to live out her faith by helping clean up before and after youth group, inviting her friends, abstaining from drinking and sex, helping her parents at home with the younger siblings, raising money for world hunger, and more. But about a year ago, this very visible and committed teenager disappeared from church. I noticed she hadn't been around and even wondered if she'd moved. It wasn't until months later—after she'd been in trouble with her parents and with the law—that she confessed to me that she'd spent those difficult months uncertain she even wanted to be a Christian anymore. During that time, she didn't care if she drank too much—in fact, she wanted to—and she didn't care if her parents found out. She no longer cared what the Bible said about God's love for her. She didn't realize what a dark time it was until she got in trouble and found out that living like an unbeliever doesn't bring all the good things it promises.

This young girl is still a leader in our youth group. She is awesome. But she reminds me that even those Christians whose confidence seems unmoving face these temptations and questions they can't quite answer. Even those who are strongest in the faith wrestle with this "it." My job as their pastor is to help them see that "it" (whatever "it" might be for them) doesn't have to control their lives. They can have freedom and peace in walking closely with Jesus.

When I was discussing this with the girls in my group, one sophomore said, "We were so good in ninth grade, little angels, and then something happened, and it all changed." Her best friend sitting next to her on the couch agreed and most of the girls in the room admitted to the same experience. The most phenomenal thing is that every girl in our group (and many others I asked online), could identify some major issue that had become a big barrier in their relationships with God during this time. "It" was something different for every girl—but they all encountered something in those years that drastically affected their lives and their faith. Usually, these issues arise as we mature and become more aware that not everyone makes the same decisions we do or believes in God as we do. "It" happens when we begin to see we are different, and we are faced with a choice to follow the crowd and its ways of living or stick to the morals we've adopted as children of God.

It's kind of like when we are children, and our parents lock the door at night. Most of us experienced this as a feeling of safety and security. Those doors kept us in, but they also kept danger away. When our parents said it was time to stay inside, we stayed inside. But as we switch over to making more of our own decisions, we know those doors can be unlocked. If we choose, we can leave our house, meet whomever we want to meet, do whatever we want to do—and deal with the consequences, whatever they may be. Autonomy or freedom from our parents is something we want, and something we hope might bring us further acceptance with our friends. But we know the doors are locked for a reason; we know they are meant to protect us. Yet we feel this struggle with "it," the call of worldly approval and false freedom that draws us away from what is truly freeing—knowing that God provides for all our needs and will give us opportunities to spread our wings when we need them.

For me, "it" was the temptation to allow guys to lead our physical relationships. I had learned at age 15 that good-looking seniors don't date naïve freshmen for the mental stimulation. I learned that if I didn't respond physically, the relationship wouldn't last long. "It" was compromising my morals to get attention from a guy I really wanted admiration from. Not compromising meant losing the relationship and maybe even being labeled. Learning to be okay with this was what conquering "it" was all about for me.

I must acknowledge that the things we struggle with as teenagers aren't always things we can change ourselves. Maybe you have experienced abuse or emotional damage from a broken adult relationship or the loss of a family member. You may have been taken advantage of, left behind, forgotten, or even neglected. Perhaps you've been pushed to the point of exhaustion by parents or other well-meaning adults who expect you to succeed in every area of life. Such situations can create unbearable pain and may leave you with low self-esteem, feelings of loneliness, inadequacy, and even helplessness. It would be unfair of me to assume that faith in God will quickly resolve these problems (although faith certainly helps). I hope you will seek help and healing. There are other books and other voices available that might do a much better job helping you through the specifics of your own struggle. But whatever trouble or challenge you are dealing with, consider the following suggestions as ways you might experience the health and wholeness God desires for you.

1. Find a friend. Talk to someone you can trust.

2. Start a journal. Use it as a place to share your thoughts and feelings.

3. Read all you can. Find writers who speak to your passions and curiosities. The collective voice of God's people can enrich your way of life.

4. Discover a place to play.

5. Allow God to heal your heart. Seek out places where God's healing can happen (church, youth group, in Bible study and meditation, in nature and God's creation). Healing may take days, months, and even years. Just remember to keep the door of your heart open to God's healing in whatever package it arrives.

There are so many manifestations of "it," so many things that promise you fulfillment but leave you with that same old sense of emptiness. What are the things that draw you in with false promises when you are weak? Shopping? Drugs? Diets? Computer relationships? Sex? Drinking? Lying? Rebelling? There are so many "its" and sometimes more than just one is lurking, ready and waiting for us when we are empty and searching.

The world around us likes to tell us that success in life is based on whom you date, what you wear, how thin or vivacious you are, whom you marry, how much money you have...when all along, God's desire is that we live in freedom. God wants to tell us we are beautiful before any guy gives his seal of approval. We are beloved before anyone includes us on the guest list for the big party. We are children of God with a great inheritance, no matter how much money or power we have here on earth.

Your beauty doesn't depend on what the scale says. God called you beautiful before you were even born! You have been fearfully and wonderfully made! Knowing this leads you to a love that will fill and complete you. And this love will lead you to love others in the same unconditional way.

YOUR CONFESSIONS

When is it hardest for you to focus on others rather than yourself?

What things about your lifestyle say, "Love me"?

What is the "it" in your life that gets in the way of knowing you are loved?

In what parts of your life do you most experience the need for love and acceptance?

LOVE YOU

Confession: Right now, one of the biggest growth areas for me in learning to love others is in the department of forgiveness. A while ago I was hurt by someone I'd genuinely trusted. It stunk. It felt awful. The command to "love your neighbor" drifted away and was replaced by "kick your neighbor in the knee"-type thoughts for me during that difficult time. Kicking or punching a person's daylights out is not something I would be good at (I have some sweet noodle arms), nor do I think it's an appropriate way to deal with someone who has hurt me— but sometimes it seems like it'd feel good to just deck the person who has caused

ME PAIN. BUT I'VE FOUND FORGIVING SOMEONE IS FAR MORE POWERFUL THAN ANY PUNCH. IT'S OFTEN THE HARDEST THING IN THE WORLD TO DO, BUT IT'S ONE IMPORTANT WAY TO LOVE OTHERS. . . FREE OF CHARGE.

"There is nothing more truly artistic than to love people."

Vincent Van Gogh

I AIN'T NO FOOL!

There's a song that was popular when I was in high school that perfectly describes how our desire to feel loved can make us lose sight of who we are. "Lovefool" by the Cardigans suggests that we can be blinded by our need to be loved—even if it isn't a real or safe or healthy love. Sensing that the object of her affection no longer cares for her, over and over the lead singer cries and pleads, "Love me, love me—say that you love me." Even if he doesn't love her, she begs him to pretend he does, to "fool" her by saying the words she longs to hear. The song reminds us that wanting to be loved (or at least, to *feel* loved) can be so distracting and so overwhelming that we become fools, losing sight of ourselves and our own power to give love.

Hearing the words "I love you" stirs so many emotions. But when these words get overused, we can forget the impact our own love can have on someone's life when we really put love in action. We speak of love so easily, but demonstrating our love is the real indication that God is working and moving in our lives. When my own desire to experience love from others took a back seat to my desire to express love for others, I knew that this God thing, this fruitful way of living, was something that would revolutionize my life and my calling. If you're ready, God can replace your intense longing to be loved and recognized with an intense desire to love others.

Is this what you seek? Or are you still a "love fool," blinded by your desire to be loved and accepted by others, rather than experiencing (and then sharing) the love God so freely offers you?

We have a natural desire to love and be loved. During our teenage years, that love is often tied up in relationships that are measured by holding hands, note passing, dating, spending time together, saying "I love you," and many other things. This urge to love someone is natural and good. However, if we're not grounded in a proper relationship to God, our desire to love and be loved can turn addictive. In our weak moments, it can cause us to do and say things that will elicit more shallow affirmation and unstable support. This is especially dangerous because we become dependent on the source of that love to satisfy our longings.

In eighth grade, I remember being so wrapped up in "loving" and "being loved" by my boyfriend that I wanted nothing but to be close to him, listen to songs about "us" on the radio, call him on the phone, go places with him, borrow his t-shirts, doodle his name on paper. There was nothing I wanted more than to be loved by him. That year we spent all our time together—which left me with less time with my girlfriends and next to no time with God. My sense of worth and all my affection came from him, and I thought he'd always be there for me.

Then came the phone call that summer. In a quiet voice, the boy I loved told me he "kind of went to a baseball game with some friends..." (Long pause.)

"I'm listening."

Then, he told me he'd kissed someone else. This news was enough to break my heart, but my dependence on him didn't allow me to hear what he was really calling to tell me. He wanted to breakup.

I couldn't believe it. I didn't understand. I was in total shock. I cried for days. My mom tried to help me by giving me some books to read, by comforting me—but nothing helped. I was freaking out. He was the one who made me believe I was loved and beautiful and amazing. Without his presence in my life I didn't have anything left.

Eventually, time eased that pain and I started hanging out with other guys. (Unfortunately, our reaction to heartbreak isn't usually a full sprint toward God for comfort and support.) I began seeking love from others to fill the space in my heart that seemed very empty. I didn't understand how this longing in my heart led me into relationships that could never satisfy my need for God. I never made the connection that a healthy heart might lead to a healthy relationship, both with God and with a future boyfriend.

The next year I ended up in the same homeroom as my ex-boyfriend. I still had strong feelings for him, but I'd been so hurt that I tried to ignore him, until he started paying attention to me again. In gym class, he asked me how I was doing. The conversation opened up the hole I'd sealed shut. I became needy again, wanting him to love me again, to see what he had missed out on. I wanted him to need me as well. Within days we were "going out" again, and my freshman year was consumed with this relationship.

I don't regret the relationship. It was fun. He was a good guy. He would never have hurt me. I loved his family and was a part of their lives. But the longer we stayed together, the more dependent I became. Dependency leaves us feeling so attached, and that attachment opened my mind and heart to saying and doing things that were emotionally and physically binding. I'd let this relationship define me for so long that I felt empty inside without it. All along there was a loving and consistent God who was ready and able to give me all the affirmation and acceptance I needed. But I chose to stay in this relationship, hurting both my boyfriend and myself in the long run.

SUMMER OF LOVE

Things changed the next summer, when my sister and I were given a chance to go to a Christian summer camp. I wouldn't say I was a Christian at that time. I was more of a pretender. I could look and act Christian if needed, but I didn't have a real relationship with Jesus.

What happened to me wasn't anything dramatic. I said a simple prayer one night, asking for forgiveness and for God to really and truly come into my life. I knew I had to make some changes in the way I was depending on others to fill my life with acceptance. I'd found a God who could fill all those holes, and I realized that staying in that relationship with my boyfriend would cause me to be more dependent on him for fulfillment, when we both needed to grow in other ways. Even though my boyfriend was a Christian who truly loved me, we had a physical bond that was too much for either one of us at that age. God wanted to purify my heart and prepare me for strong relationships. But that wouldn't happen until I stopped depending on everyone else to fulfill my longings and needs.

LOVE YOU

Have you ever been in a relationship like this? It doesn't have to be a boyfriend. The same thing can happen with a best friend, if we base our worth on what that person thinks or says about us. We build up dependency so easily and so quickly that we miss out on all of the promises God wants to share with us.

When God tells us who we are in Christ, when God calls us beloved and fills our lives with fruit, we become free to be ourselves. We become confident in who we are and stop putting on masks or performing for other people to gain their approval. When this happens in us, something else miraculous happens. We free others to be who they are as well! We give others the opportunity to take off their own masks and understand who they really are (without focusing on gaining our approval).

When you are so close to God that you are okay with who you are and okay with people around you (differences and all!), then you are truly free to love others. It's easy to love our friends when they make us happy or make us feel good about ourselves. But what about the times when your friends act weird, immature, or embarrass you? What about when they hurt you or disrespect you? It's so hard to love when it seems like everyone is only thinking of himself or herself. This is where your faith comes in. Secure in God's love and who you are, you become the example and the revelation of God to others. When your sense of worth comes from God and when the fruit of love, joy, peace, patience, kindness, goodness, faithfulness, gentleness, and self-control fills your heart with purpose, you will find all kinds of ways to love even the most unlovable people.

Moving from a life that cries out "love me, love me!" to a life built around loving God and others can't be done using some kit you order online. It comes from an indwelling of God's Spirit that comes when you trust God to fill your life with good things. It's a way of life that springs from having God's truth in your heart and God's forgiveness in your soul.

God's nature is constant. Christ's character is unchanging. Love as described in the Bible is consistent—always patient and kind, never jealous or boastful. (Check out 1 Corinthians 13 to read Paul's wonderful description of love.) There isn't any confusion about love's intentions, which are always pure.

But we get this idea—often from relationships that begin in our teenage years—that love is something you pay for, something you have to earn and, likewise, something others have to earn from you. This couldn't be further from the nature of real love. You have a special gift to offer to everyone who passes through your life. This gift is the unwavering ability to offer love even when it's not deserved.

Think about a person in your life who causes you a lot of grief. Maybe it is someone at school, or at work, or even at home. What might your relationship look like if you showed that person love even when he or she had fallen short?

There is a secret tucked gently in the pages of 1 John that tells us just how powerful loving someone is. 1 John 4:12 begins with a plain truth that we already know ("No one has ever seen God"), but then it lets us in on a reality that has the power to revolutionize our world: "If we love one another, God lives in us and his love is made complete in us." Basically, God can be seen, revealed, and experienced as we love other people. God can be seen in your house, in your car, in your school, in your community, and in your world. God is visible anywhere we are willing to express love.

To me this is a mind-blowing concept! Ever since I became a Christian, I've wanted the world to be able to see God at work, to see God's grace and mercy, to see God's face. And now I know it's possible, because when we love one another, we give people an opportunity to see God in us. I'm astonished to be writing a book for people who have an amazing power—the power to reveal the face of God to our world!

That kind of power puts each of us in a position of great responsibility. It's the responsibility of being a "supermodel." We are to share and model the love of Christ. If we don't love others, God's face and character won't be known where we live. But imagine what the world would be like if every one of us embraced this call to love others. Imagine how much more we would know and become like our creator God!

We miss out on a huge blessing when we focus on getting rather than giving. Secure in the knowledge that we are God's beloved, we are free to love others, And as we share God's love, we find true fulfillment.

Natasha Bedingfield's song "These Words" offers an alternative to our "love-foolish" desire to always feel loved by others. Throughout the song, the same phrase is repeated over and over again, "I love you, I love you, I love you." Can you sing these words? Even better, does your life sing these words? God can move you from merely saying these words to a place where you, filled with the love of Jesus, are able to live them out and truly care for those around you. It's then, when we've learned what it means to love, that we really become supermodels.

YOUR CONFESSIONS

Have you ever been dependent on anyone to satisfy your need to feel loved? If so, who?

What's it like when someone you love (and who loves you) lets you down?

Why is it important to receive love from God first?

How can God be made visible in your world—at home, at church, in school, with friends?

Take some time to read over the book of 1 John. (It's a short book—only four chapters.) Write down your favorite verse.

Ask God to help you receive his love, and know that it is all you need.

Thank God by giving love to those around you. The organizations and opportunities below are just a small sampling of the many ways you can live out God's love for others.

Local Opportunities to Love:

Serve meals at an area soup kitchen or homeless shelter.
Volunteer at a local hospital or nursing home.
Take part in a short-term mission trip.
Hold a "See You at the Pole" prayer event at your public school (www.syatp.com).
Spend time with foster children at a local foster care facility.

Global Opportunities to Love:

30 Hour Famine (www.30hourfamine.org)
One Life Revolution (www.onelife.org)
Invisible Children (www.invisiblechildren.com)
The Amazing Change (www.theamazingchange.com)

THAT'S WHAT DREAMS ARE MADE OF...

CONFESSION: I WAS SAD DURING MY FINAL MOMENTS AS MISS PARADE OF THE HILLS. THE YEAR WAS BIZARRE, BUT IT WAS ALSO ONE OF THE BIGGEST BLESSINGS OF MY HIGH SCHOOL LIFE. I HOPE TO GIVE MY BRACELET WITH THE CHARMS REPRESENTING ALL OF THE FESTIVALS I ATTENDED TO MY DAUGHTER SOMEDAY. I WANT HER TO KNOW THAT EVEN THE SMALLEST THINGS CAN AMOUNT TO BIG DREAMS COMING TRUE.

So by now it's pretty obvious I didn't become a supermodel exactly as I'd imagined when I was a child. I did spend a year as a festival queen, but it was a far cry from the glamorous supermodel lifestyle I'd envisioned.

But just because I didn't become a supermodel like I'd hoped, that doesn't mean my dream didn't come true. I've become a supermodel in a very different way. As a youth pastor, I try to be a model for the girls I work with. I'm not perfect; in fact, I tend to fall in the "reject camp" quite often! But there are always girls who need a friend—someone who has been through similar situations and can relate to their needs. Over the past six years I've had the blessing of getting to be a part of the lives of many teenage girls through friendship and ministry. A formal modeling career could never have delivered the kind of life-changing moments I've had the honor of being a part of. I have loved (and still love!) so many wonderful young women. They have made me a better person. They have changed my life for good.

My very first job as a youth minister was at a little church in Orlando, Florida. It didn't take long for me to see that the relationships I would form while there would affect me for a lifetime. Not every girl I met and ministered to ended up on the right path. A few of them struggled with huge problems, addictions, and fears. Some of them even ended up running away from home. I tried my best to love each of these girls, but in some cases the challenges seemed to get the best of them. At first, I felt like a failure, like the time I spent with them wasn't making a difference. That feeling changed when I started hearing back from some of the girls years later. What mattered to them was that I was there and willing to listen. I didn't have the answers for all their struggles, only the promise that God wouldn't leave them and that they could always call me if they needed anything. But my efforts to express God's love and kindness made a much bigger difference than I realized.

Being a supermodel isn't about having it all together. It isn't about gaining perfection in every way. It's about living each day knowing that other people may need you...that other people are watching...and that other people matter. Jesus came to forgive us of our sins, to cleanse the dirt from our lives, but he didn't pay such a huge price just so we could go to heaven after we die. Heaven starts here on earth when we live out the dreams God gives us, love one another, and keep Christ at the center of our lives.

My second youth group in Rockledge, Florida, was made up of students who had been without a youth pastor for a few years. They were ready for someone to adopt them and model Christlikeness to them. When I first arrived as their new youth pastor, some of them were weirded out that I was a woman—their previous youth pastors were all men. That took some getting used to. But as the days and weeks passed, we fell in love. Not the romantic kind of love, but we started loving each other—mess-ups and all. I made some mistakes with them. I picked my nose way too often in front of them. I got hyper after guys who wouldn't change their socks. But they loved me anyway! They goofed off and broke things sometimes. They made messes after I'd just cleaned up. They got in disagreements and hurt one another's feelings sometimes, and I'd have to mediate. But I loved them anyway. There were times when they didn't listen to me, and times when I didn't listen to them. But something beautiful happened during those years. We learned to be okay with who we are as individuals. I was a "supermodel" for them—and they were "supermodels" for me.

The same is true at the church where I currently work in Southlake, Texas. I'm surrounded by hundreds of students who choose God and loving others over their own needs. When teens in my youth group got excited about the Invisible Children campaign, I saw Jesus here in Southlake. When they raised over

$20,000 to feed children through the 30-Hour Famine, I saw Jesus in their hearts. When they set up for youth group and take out the trash, I see servants modeling Christ's message in our church. It's amazing when the fruit starts growing. It's contagious, it's exciting, and it's a beautiful thing.

The fruit of the Spirit is still growing in my life and changing me, not because of any good in me, but because of the good in God who offers these gifts. The Holy Spirit's work in my life is something no runway could deliver. No magazine photo spread could compare to its significance and influence on my life. I hope it is the same for you. Once you've tasted the fruit, you are going to want more.

I remember a very special summer vacation I spent with my friend Karen in Mullet Lake (near Mackinac Island, Michigan). We were at her grandma's lake house, sitting on the dock with our feet in the water, when we were called inside to eat. I was a finicky eater who always worried about what kind of food would be served at each meal. On this day, Karen's grandma had prepared a light meal of fruit salad. It may be hard to believe, but I'd never eaten fruit salad before. And I wasn't very hopeful—since the only fruit I knew I liked at the time were apples and grapes.

I didn't want to be rude, and I didn't want to be hungry, so I gave the fruit salad a shot. What I experienced that summer day was something completely new, delicious, refreshing, and wonderful. I never knew that watermelon, kiwi, grapes, apples, and cantaloupe could taste so good together! It was so good and so fulfilling—better than I could ever have imagined.

This is how our faith can be. God can fill our lives with so many good things. God can give us all we need to pursue our dreams with peace and courage. God can give us special gifts and graces to love others along the way. All we have to do is open our lives to God's love.

I look around at all the young ladies in my life. I see dreams and potential. I see fears and timid hearts. I see playful friends and bright spirits. I see hurting home lives and broken relationships. I see loving sisters and hope-filled friends. I see bad timing and difficult circumstances. I see girls who have dreams, but they are often afraid they'll be left alone to fail if they try.

Two of the most special young women in my life are my sisters, Courtney and Betsy.

Courtney is eight years younger than me. When she was growing up, she would wear every plastic Avon necklace she owned (all at the same time). She would cake on bright pink lipstick, play dress up, and sing country music in my old pageant dress while looking at her reflection in the kitchen oven. Courtney had big dreams as a little girl, and she still does. Not everything has gone as planned. She's had some struggles and broken dreams along the way. But I see her living life with a spirit of hope. Her dreams have been reinvented by a loving God who can make all things new. She continues to chase her dreams, and I believe with all my heart that she is making a difference for God. She is a supermodel of hope to others who see how she has risen above her difficult circumstances to a really joyful and fulfilled life.

My other sister, Betsy, is only a year and a half younger than me. When we were teenagers, she went to a youth conference and developed a passion for world missions. God put big dreams in her heart. By the time she was 18 years old, she'd already traveled as a missionary to four or five different countries. She used to speak of her experiences in places like Thailand, India, and Vietnam, telling us all about how much God was changing her heart so she could share his word with a lost world. Her dream was to go wherever God sent her and to love the unloved. I imagined Betsy's dream would lead her to live the rest of her life in a foreign country; she probably thought the same. But today (for now, anyway), she lives in Ohio with her husband and children. Ohio is much different from Lebanon (where she once worked as a nanny) or Thailand (where she hugged and shared God's love with street children). She may not be ministering to people in impoverished countries as she'd imagined. But her dream is still very much alive—in the stories she tells, the goals she has, and the way she loves those around her. She continues to be a supermodel for me. The shape of her dreams has changed, but the spirit of those dreams is alive. I see it alive in the way she raises her son and daughter. I see it alive in the things she cares about. I see it alive when she gives even when she doesn't have much to give.

You have dreams that God has placed in your mind and heart. Your dreams are not exactly like anyone else's dreams, because we are all different, sacred, and made in the image of our Creator who was the biggest dreamer of all. Even if you think your dreams are completely out of reach, remember that God can help you achieve the dreams he has given you. The dream you live out may not look exactly the way you imagined it. But with God's help, you'll learn to see in different ways. If you picked up this book looking for a reason to believe again, I pray that the Holy Spirit will fill your heart and give you the confidence to move forward.

My heart is full of emotions as I finish up the last chapter of this book and prepare to send it off to the publisher. I've recently begun living out a dream that's brand new to me. Seven days ago I gave birth to a beautiful baby girl. Her name is Kirra, and her arrival makes the content I've shared in this book even more important to me. I want Kirra to know how beloved she is. I can't even imagine a day when she might come home feeling hurt by the world and its judgments—but I know those days will come for her. It's impossible to walk through life without some trials. But I am certain that God knows and loves Kirra (just as God knows and loves each of us) and will hold her close through the good times and the bad times. God has given her many promises (the same ones given to you and me).

As I look at my newborn daughter, I know that Kirra will dream her very own dreams. Kirra's dreams will probably be very different from my own. She may have my eyes and her daddy's toes, but her dreams will be entirely her own. Coy and I will give her many things as her parents, but her dreams will come from her heart, from her personality, from her God-given gifts and passions. With our love, help, and support, I pray she will hold onto God and then pursue with wild abandon the dreams that fill her soul. This is my prayer for Kirra, and it's also my prayer for you.

My life as a supermodel is a day-by-day walk across the runway of life. I'm living my dreams today as a child of God, a wife, a mother, a daughter, a sister, a youth pastor, and a friend. There are times when I struggle, but God gives me what I need each day, whether it be an extra dose of love, patience, kindness, or self-control...whatever it is, God provides.

CONFESSIONS OF A Not-So-SUPERMODEL

So by God's grace, I'm a supermodel of faith. I've shared these stories and confessions hoping you'll let God fill your life with fruit as you pursue the dreams growing in your heart. It's guaranteed you'll have to overcome many obstacles along the way. But God has promised never to leave you and to give you strength when you are tired.

I hope you'll never give up on that passion that burns in your heart. I've been blessed to see many of my own dreams fulfilled, and I'm already dreaming again of things to come and new ways to transform our world with the compassion and love of Christ. When all our dreams are joined together, we have the ability to bring great hope and healing to our world.

So keep dreaming girls. God's got your back as you go after the dreams of your life. Christ is with us as we go on this supermodel journey of faith.

This book is about finding the joy only God can give. You'll study the book of Philippians and learn great stuff about how the Holy Spirit helps believers find real happiness despite what's going on in their lives or in their heads.

Secret Power to Joy, Becoming a Star, and Great Hair Days
A Personal Bible Study on the Book of Philippians
Susie Shellenberger
RETAIL $9.99
ISBN 0-310-25678-X

This book will help you figure out what does and doesn't fit with being a Christian. You can do this study at your own pace by yourself, with a friend, or with a bunch of friends.

Secret Power to Treasures, Purity, and a Good Complexion
A Personal Bible Study on the Book of Colossians
Susie Shellenberger
RETAIL $9.99
ISBN 0-310-25679-8

Through true-to-life anecdotes and fun assignments, students will come to realize that happiness and success come by dressing themselves with the chapionship attire that's theirs because of what Jesus did on the cross.

Secret Power to Winning, Happiness, and a Cool Wardrobe
A Personal Bible Study on the Book of 1 Peter
Susie Shellenberger
RETAIL $9.99
ISBN 0-310-25680-1

This fun and engaging study on the book of Ruth will help teenage girls understand what faith and hope are all about, and how they play out in their lives—yes, even in their love lives. Designed for busy girls, this book works equally well as a solo or group study

Secret Power to Faith, Family, and Getting a Guy
A Personal Bible Study on the Book of Ruth
Susie Shellenberger
RETAIL $9.99
ISBN 0-310-25677-9

invert

Visit www.invertbooks.com or your local bookstore.

Many people think teenagers aren't capable of much. But Zach Hunter is proving those people wrong. He's only fifteen, but he's working to end slavery in the world—and he's making changes that affect millions of people. Find out how Zach is making a difference and how you can make changes in the things that you see wrong with our world.

Be the Change
Your Guide to Freeing Slaves and Changing the World
Zach Hunter
RETAIL $9.99
ISBN 0-310-27756-6

How do you see yourself? How does God see you? Super models, postive thinking, self-help books, diets, cosmetics, dating guides—they are all suppposed to make you more self-assured. But they often wind up leading to confusion, disappointment, and insecurity.

Secret Power for Girls
Identity, Security, and Self-Respect in Troubling Times
Susie Shellenberger
RETAIL $9.99
ISBN 0-310-24972-4

invert

Visit www.invertbooks.com or your local bookstore.

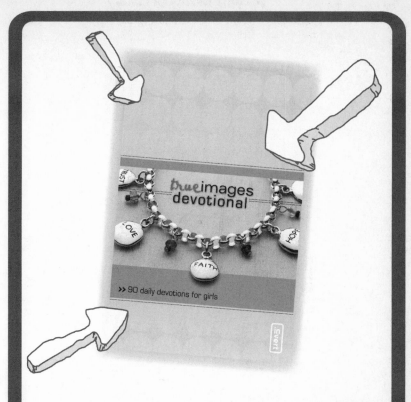

What is true beauty? Learn what it means to develop lasting inner beauty, the kind that God desires for you! By spending time in God's Word each day, you'll understand more about being the beautiful young woman God created you to be. Each devotion contains a Bible verse, a thought for the day, further reading, a prayer, and space to journal your thoughts.

True Images Devotional
90 Daily Devotions for Girls
Author Name
RETAIL $12.99
ISBN 0-310-26705-8

ENJOY THE SILENCE

A 30 DAY EXPERIMENT
IN LISTENING TO GOD

MAGGIE ROBBINS
DUFFY ROBBINS

invert

It's not that kids don't want to read the Bible, it's that they may not know how. *Enjoy the Silence's* 30 guided exercises plug your students into the ancient discipline of Lectio Divina. Each lesson provides a selection of Scripture, prompts for meditation, a chance to listen to God, and a way to respond to what they've read.

Enjoy the Silence
A 30 Day Experiment in Listening to God
Duffy Robbins and Maggie Robbins
RETAIL $9.99
ISBN 0-310-25991-6

Visit www.invertbooks.com or your local bookstore.